FAMILY ISSUES IN THE 21ST CENTURY

ADOPTION RECORDS AND POSTADOPTION CONTACT AGREEMENTS

STATE STATUTES

FAMILY ISSUES IN THE 21ST CENTURY

Additional books in this series can be found on Nova's website
under the Series tab.

Additional e-books in this series can be found on Nova's website
under the eBooks tab.

FAMILY ISSUES IN THE 21ST CENTURY

ADOPTION RECORDS AND POSTADOPTION CONTACT AGREEMENTS

STATE STATUTES

EBONY BARTLETT
EDITOR

New York

Copyright © 2016 by Nova Science Publishers, Inc.

All rights reserved. No part of this book may be reproduced, stored in a retrieval system or transmitted in any form or by any means: electronic, electrostatic, magnetic, tape, mechanical photocopying, recording or otherwise without the written permission of the Publisher.

We have partnered with Copyright Clearance Center to make it easy for you to obtain permissions to reuse content from this publication. Simply navigate to this publication's page on Nova's website and locate the "Get Permission" button below the title description. This button is linked directly to the title's permission page on copyright.com. Alternatively, you can visit copyright.com and search by title, ISBN, or ISSN.

For further questions about using the service on copyright.com, please contact:
Copyright Clearance Center
Phone: +1-(978) 750-8400   Fax: +1-(978) 750-4470   E-mail: info@copyright.com.

NOTICE TO THE READER

The Publisher has taken reasonable care in the preparation of this book, but makes no expressed or implied warranty of any kind and assumes no responsibility for any errors or omissions. No liability is assumed for incidental or consequential damages in connection with or arising out of information contained in this book. The Publisher shall not be liable for any special, consequential, or exemplary damages resulting, in whole or in part, from the readers' use of, or reliance upon, this material. Any parts of this book based on government reports are so indicated and copyright is claimed for those parts to the extent applicable to compilations of such works.

Independent verification should be sought for any data, advice or recommendations contained in this book. In addition, no responsibility is assumed by the publisher for any injury and/or damage to persons or property arising from any methods, products, instructions, ideas or otherwise contained in this publication.

This publication is designed to provide accurate and authoritative information with regard to the subject matter covered herein. It is sold with the clear understanding that the Publisher is not engaged in rendering legal or any other professional services. If legal or any other expert assistance is required, the services of a competent person should be sought. FROM A DECLARATION OF PARTICIPANTS JOINTLY ADOPTED BY A COMMITTEE OF THE AMERICAN BAR ASSOCIATION AND A COMMITTEE OF PUBLISHERS.

Additional color graphics may be available in the e-book version of this book.

Library of Congress Cataloging-in-Publication Data

ISBN: 978-1-63485-437-5

Published by Nova Science Publishers, Inc. † New York

CONTENTS

Preface		**vii**
Chapter 1	Access to Adoption Records *Child Welfare Information Gateway*	**1**
Chapter 2	Postadoption Contact Agreements between Birth and Adoptive Families *Child Welfare Information Gateway*	**111**
Index		**185**

PREFACE

In nearly all States, adoption records are sealed and withheld from public inspection after an adoption is finalized. This book discusses state laws that provide for access to both nonidentifying and identifying information from an adoption record by adoptive parents and adult adopted persons, while still protecting the interests of all parties. Furthermore, the book discusses postadoption contact agreements, which are arrangements that allow contact between a child's adoptive family and members of the child's birth family or other persons with whom the child has an established relationship, such as a foster parent, after the child's adoption has been finalized. These arrangements, sometimes referred to as cooperative adoption or open adoption agreements, can range from informal, mutual understandings between the birth and adoptive families to written, formal contracts.

In: Adoption Records …
Editor: Ebony Bartlett

ISBN: 978-1-63485-437-5
© 2016 Nova Science Publishers, Inc.

Chapter 1

ACCESS TO ADOPTION RECORDS[*]

Child Welfare Information Gateway

In nearly all States, adoption records are sealed and withheld from public inspection after an adoption is finalized. Most States have instituted procedures by which parties to an adoption may obtain both nonidentifying and identifying information from an adoption record while still protecting the interests of all parties.

WHAT'S INSIDE

Nonidentifying information
Restrictions on release of nonidentifying information
Identifying information
Mutual consent registries
Other methods of obtaining consent
Access to an original birth certificate
Summaries of State laws

To find statute information for a particular State, go to
https://www.childwelfare. gov/topics/systemwide/ laws-policies/state/.

---

[*] This is an edited, reformatted and augmented version of a document issued by the U.S. Department of Health and Human Services, Children's Bureau, 2016. State statute summaries are current through June 2015.

NONIDENTIFYING INFORMATION

Nonidentifying information generally is limited to descriptive details about an adopted person and the adopted person's birth relatives. This type of information generally is provided to the adopting parents at the time of the adoption. Nonidentifying information may include the following:

- Date and place of the adopted person's birth
- Age of the birth parents and general physical description, such as eye and hair color
- Race, ethnicity, religion, and medical history of the birth parents
- Educational level of the birth parents and their occupations at the time of the adoption
- Reason for placing the child for adoption
- Existence of other children born to each birth parent

All States and American Samoa have provisions in statutes that allow access to nonidentifying information by an adoptive parent or a guardian of an adopted person who is still a minor. Nearly all States allow the adopted person to access nonidentifying information about birth relatives, generally upon written request. Usually, the adopted person must be at least age 18 before he or she may access this information.[1]

Approximately 26 States allow birth parents access to nonidentifying information, generally about the health and social history of the child.[2] In addition, 15 States give such access to adult birth siblings.[3] Policies on what information is collected and how that information is maintained and disclosed vary from State to State.

RESTRICTIONS ON RELEASE OF NONIDENTIFYING INFORMATION

Some jurisdictions are more restrictive about the release of information from adoption records. New York, Oklahoma, and Rhode Island require the person seeking nonidentifying information to register with the State adoption registry. In Pennsylvania, nonidentifying information is available through a registry or the court or agency that handled the adoption. Guam requires a party to petition the court before any information can be released.

Access to Adoption Records

Nonidentifying information that is generally available includes medical and health information about the child and the child's birth family at the time of the adoptive placement. Alabama, Illinois, Kansas, Maryland, Minnesota, Mississippi, and Wyoming statutes allow adoptive parents to request that the State adoption registry contact birth parents when additional health information is medically necessary. In Georgia, any medical information about the birth family that is received by the department or child-placing agency must be provided to the adoptive parents or adult adopted person.

IDENTIFYING INFORMATION

Identifying information is information from the disclosure of adoption records or elsewhere that may lead to the positive identification of birth parents, the adopted person, or other birth relatives. Identifying information may include current or past names of the person, addresses, employment, or other similar records or information. Statutes in nearly all States permit the release of identifying information when the person whose information is sought has consented to the release.[4] If consent is not on file with the appropriate entity, the information may not be released without a court order documenting good cause to release the information. A person seeking a court order must be able to demonstrate by clear and convincing evidence that there is a compelling reason for disclosure that outweighs maintaining the confidentiality of a party to an adoption.[5]

Access to information is not always restricted to birth parents and adopted persons. Approximately 37 States allow biological siblings of the adopted person to seek and release identifying information upon mutual consent.[6]

Some States have imposed limitations on the release of identifying information. Arkansas, Mississippi, South Carolina, and Texas require the adopted person to undergo counseling about the process and potential implications of search and contact with his or her birth family before any information is disclosed. In Connecticut, release of identifying information is prohibited if the department or child-placing agency that possesses the information determines that the requested information would be "seriously disruptive to or endanger the physical or emotional health of the person whose identity is being requested."[7]

MUTUAL CONSENT REGISTRIES

A mutual consent registry is one method many States use to arrange the consents that are required for release of identifying information. A mutual consent registry is a means for individuals directly involved in adoptions to indicate their willingness or unwillingness to have their identifying information disclosed. Approximately 30 States have established some form of a mutual consent registry.[8]

Procedures for mutual consent registries vary significantly from State to State. Most registries require consent of at least one birth parent and an adopted person over the age of 18 or 21, or of adoptive parents if the adopted person is a minor, in order to release identifying information. Most States that have registries require the parties seeking to exchange information to file affidavits consenting to the release of their personal information. However, eight States will release information from the registry upon request unless the affected party has filed an affidavit requesting nondisclosure.[9]

OTHER METHODS OF OBTAINING CONSENT

States that have not established registries may use alternative methods for disclosing identifying information. Search and consent procedures authorize a public or private agency to assist a party in locating birth family members to determine if they consent to the release of information. Some States have a search and consent procedure called a confidential intermediary system.[10] With this system, an individual called a confidential intermediary is certified by the court to have access to sealed adoption records for the purpose of conducting a search for birth family members to obtain their consent for contact. Other States use an affidavit system through which birth family members can either file their consent to release identifying information or to register their refusal to be contacted or to release identifying information.[11] The written permission may be referred to as a consent, waiver, or authorization form.

ACCESS TO AN ORIGINAL BIRTH CERTIFICATE

When an adoption is finalized, a new birth certificate for the child is customarily issued to the adoptive parents. The original birth certificate is then sealed and kept confidential by the State registrar of vital records. In the past, nearly all States required adopted persons to obtain a court order to gain access to their original birth certificates. In approximately 25 States, the District of Columbia, American Samoa, Guam, and Puerto Rico, a court order is still required.[12] However, in many States, the laws are changing to allow easier access to these records. Some of the means for providing information access include:

- Through a court order when all parties have consented[13]
- At the request of the adult adopted person[14]
- At the request of the adopted person, unless the birth parent has filed an affidavit denying release of confidential records[15]
- When eligibility to receive identifying information has been established with a State adoption registry[16]
- When consents from the birth parents to release identifying information are on file[17]

WHERE INFORMATION CAN BE LOCATED

To find contact information for a State agency or department that assists in accessing adoption records, go to Child Welfare Information Gateway's National Foster Care and Adoption Directory and search under Accessing Adoption Records at https://www.childwelfare.gov/nfcad/.

See the Adoption Search and Reunion section of the Child Welfare Information Gateway website at https:// www.childwelfare.gov/topics/ adoption/search/ for more information on searching for birth relatives, including a link to the International Soundex Reunion, a free mutual consent reunion registry for people seeking birth relatives at http://www.isrr.net/.

6　　　　　　Child Welfare Information Gateway

> This publication is a product of the State Statutes Series prepared by Child Welfare Information Gateway. While every attempt has been made to be complete, additional information on these topics may be in other sections of a State's code as well as agency regulations, case law, and informal practices and procedures.

Alabama

Who May Access Information
Citation: Ala. Code § 26-10A-31
Nonidentifying information may be released, upon request, to:

- The adoptive parents
- The birth parents
- The adopted person who is age 19 or older

Only the adult adopted person may access identifying information.
Access to Nonidentifying Information
Citation: Ala. Code § 26-10A-31
Nonidentifying information is limited to:

- The health and medical history of birth parents and the adopted person
- General family background
- Physical descriptions
- The length of time the child was in out-of-home care other than with the adoptive parents
- The circumstances resulting in the adoption

If the court finds that any person has a compelling need for nonidentifying information that can be obtained only through contact with the adopted person, the birth parents, or the adoptive parents, the court shall direct the agency or a mutually agreed upon intermediary to establish contact with the adopted person, the birth parents, or the adoptive parents in order to obtain the information needed without disclosing identifying information. The information then shall be filed with the court and released to the applicant at the discretion of the court. The identity and whereabouts of the person or persons contacted shall remain confidential.

Access to Adoption Records   7

Mutual Access to Identifying Information
Citation: Ala. Code § 26-10A-31

If either birth parent has given consent in writing for disclosure of identifying information, the State Department of Human Resources or a licensed child-placing agency shall release such identifying information.

When an adopted person reaches age 19, he or she may petition the court for the disclosure of identifying information if the birth parent has not previously given consent. The court shall direct an intermediary to contact the birth parents to determine if they will consent to the release of identifying information. If the birth parents consent to the release of identifying information, the court shall order its release. If the birth parents are deceased, cannot be found, or do not consent, the court shall weigh the interest and rights of all of the parties and determine if the identifying information should be released without the consent of the birth parents.

Access to Original Birth Certificate
Citation: Ala. Code § 22-9A-12(c)-(d)

Any person age 19 or older who was born in Alabama and who has had an original birth certificate removed from the files due to an adoption may, upon written request, receive a copy of that birth certificate and any evidence of the adoption held with the original record.

A birth parent at any time may request from the State Registrar of Vital Statistics a contact preference form that shall accompany a birth certificate. The contact preference form shall indicate one of the following:

- He or she would like to be contacted.
- He or she would prefer to be contacted only through an intermediary.
- He or she would prefer not to be contacted at this time, but may submit an updated contact preference at a later time.

A medical history form shall be supplied to the birth parent upon request of a contact preference form. The medical history form and the contact preference form are confidential communications from the birth parent to the person named on the sealed birth certificate and shall be placed in a sealed envelope upon receipt from the birth parent. The sealed envelope shall be released to a person requesting his or her own original birth certificate.

Where the Information Can Be Located

- Alabama Department of Public Health, Birth Certificates
- The licensed investigating agency appointed by the court per § 26-10A-19(b), (c)

Alaska

Who May Access Information
Citation: Alaska Code § 18.50.500
Identifying information may be accessed by:
- The adopted person who is age 18 or older
- The birth parent

The adoptive parent may access nonidentifying information.
Access to Nonidentifying Information
Citation: Alaska Code § 18.50.510
The State Registrar may release information regarding the birth parents at the request of an adoptive parent or an adopted person who is age 18 or older. Nonidentifying information includes:

- The age of the birth parents at the child's birth
- The birth parents' heritage, including ethnic background and Tribal membership
- The medical history of the birth parents and blood relatives of the birth parents
- The number of years of school completed by the birth parents when the child was born
- The physical description of the birth parents at the child's birth, including height, weight, and color of eyes, hair, and skin
- The existence of other children of the birth parents
- The religion of the birth parents
- Whether the birth parent was alive at the time of the adoption
- Other information provided by the birth parents for disclosure to the child, including photos and letters

Access to Adoption Records

Mutual Access to Identifying Information
Citation: Alaska Code § 18.50.500

The State Registrar shall disclose to a birth parent, at that parent's request, the most current name and address of an adopted child as they appear in the State Registrar's adoption files, if the child is 18 or older and has requested in writing that the information be disclosed if ever requested by the birth parent.

Access to Original Birth Certificate
Citation: Alaska Code § 18.50.500

After receiving a request for the identity of a birth parent by an adopted person who is age 18 or older, the State Registrar shall provide the person with an uncertified copy of the person's original birth certificate and any changes in the birth parent's name or address attached to the certificate.

An adopted person age 18 or older or a birth parent may submit to the State registrar a notice of change of name or address. The State registrar shall attach the information to the original birth certificate of the adopted person.

Where the Information Can Be Located

Bureau of Vital Statistics, Alaska Department of Health and Social Services

American Samoa

Who May Access Information
Citation: Ann. Code § 45.0414

Any party to an adoption proceeding may see the written report filed by the Department of Health or child-placing agency.

Access to Nonidentifying Information
Citation: Ann. Code § 45.0414

Accessible nonidentifying information includes the child's family background and reasons for the adoption.

Mutual Access to Identifying Information
Citation: Ann. Code § 45.0414

The names of the birth parents and the adoptive parents, and any means of identifying either, are not available except upon order of the court.

Access to Original Birth Certificate
Citation: Ann. Code § 45.0424

The original birth certificate is sealed and may not be released without a court order.

10   Child Welfare Information Gateway

Where the Information Can Be Located
American Samoa Government, Office of Vital Statistics

Arizona

Who May Access Information
Citation: Rev. Stat. § 8-129
The following persons may have access to family information:

* The adoptive parents or a guardian of the adopted person
* The adopted person who is age 18 or older
* If the adopted person has died, the adopted person's spouse if he or she is the legal parent of the adopted person's child, or the guardian of any child of the adopted person
* If the adopted person has died, any child of the adopted person who is age 18 or older
* The birth parents or other birth children of the birth parents

Access to Nonidentifying Information
Citation: Rev. Stat. §§ 8-121; 8-129
Nonidentifying information may be released upon request to any of the persons listed above. Nonidentifying information may include the health and genetic history of the birth parents and members of the birth parents' families.

Mutual Access to Identifying Information
Citation: Rev. Stat. § 8-121
Court personnel, the division, an attorney assisting in a direct placement adoption, or an agency may provide partial or complete identifying information between a birth parent and adoptive parent when the parties mutually agree to share specific identifying information and make a written request to the court, the division, or the agency.

A person may petition the court to obtain information relating to an adoption that is in the possession of the court, the division, or any agency or attorney involved in the adoption. The court shall not release identifying information unless the person requesting the information has established a compelling need for disclosure or consent has been obtained.

An adopted person age 18 or older or a birth parent may file at any time a notarized statement granting consent, withholding consent, or withdrawing a consent previously given for the release of confidential information with the

Access to Adoption Records

court and the agency, division, or attorney who participated in the adoption. If an adopted person who is 18 or older and the birth mother or birth father have filed consent to the release of confidential information, the court may disclose the information, except identifying information relating to a birth parent who did not grant written consent.

Access to Original Birth Certificate
Citation: Rev. Stat. § 36-337
The original birth certificate can be made available only upon a court order or as prescribed by rule.

Where the Information Can Be Located
Arizona Confidential Intermediary Program, Arizona Supreme Court

Arkansas

Who May Access Information
Citation: Ann. Code §§ 9-9-504; 9-9-505
Nonidentifying information is available to:

- The adoptive parents of the child or the child's guardian
- The adopted person
- If the adopted person has died, the adopted person's children, widow or widower, or the guardian of any child of the adopted person
- The birth parent of the adopted person
- Any child welfare agency having custody of the adopted person

Access to identifying information is available to the adult adopted person, the birth parents, and any person related within the second degree through the Adoption Registry.

Access to Nonidentifying Information
Citation: Ann. Code § 9-9-505
Nonidentifying information is available upon request to any person listed above. Nonidentifying information includes the health, genetic, and social history of the child.

Mutual Access to Identifying Information
Citation: Ann. Code § 9-9-504
A person eligible to register may request the disclosure of identifying information by filing an affidavit with the adoption registry that includes the following:

12 Child Welfare Information Gateway

- The person's current name and address
- Any previous name by which the applicant was known
- The original and adopted names, if known, of the adopted person
- The place and date of birth of the adopted person
- The name and address of the adoption agency or other entity, organization, or person placing the adopted person, if known

The applicant shall notify the registry of any change in name or location that occurs subsequent to his or her filing of the affidavit. The registry shall have no duty to search for an applicant who fails to register his or her most recent address.

The administrator of the mutual consent voluntary adoption registry shall process each affidavit in an attempt to match the adult adopted person and the birth parents or other relatives. The processing shall include research from agency records, when available, and when agency records are not available, research from court records to determine conclusively whether the applicants match.

The administrator shall determine that there is a match when the adult adopted person and a birth parent or other relative have filed affidavits with the adoption registry and have each received the required counseling.

Access to Original Birth Certificate
Citation: Ann. Code § 20-18-406
The original birth certificate is available only upon a court order or as provided by regulation.

Where the Information Can Be Located

- Arkansas Mutual Consent Voluntary Adoption Registry
- The licensed agency involved in the adoption

California

Who May Access Information
Citation: Fam. Code § 9202; 9203
Nonidentifying information is available to:

- The adopted person who is age 18 or older
- The adoptive parent of an adopted person who is under age 18

Identifying information is available to:

- The adopted person who is age 21 or older
- The birth parent of an adult adopted person
- The adoptive parent of an adopted person who is under age 21

Access to Nonidentifying Information
Citation: Fam. Code §§ 8706; 8817; 9202
Nonidentifying information about the birth parents and adopted person, such as medical history, scholastic information, psychological evaluations, and developmental history, is provided to the adopting parents.

The department or licensed adoption agency shall provide a copy of the medical report, in the manner the department prescribes by regulation, to any of the following persons upon the person's request:

- A person who has been adopted who is at least age 18 or presents a certified copy of the person's marriage certificate
- The adoptive parent of a person under age 18

A person who is denied access to a medical report may petition the court for review of the reasonableness of the department's or licensed adoption agency's decision.

The names and addresses of any persons contained in the report shall be removed unless the person requesting the report has previously received the information.

Mutual Access to Identifying Information
Citation: Fam. Code §§ 9201; 9203; 9205; 9206
The adopted person who is 21 or older may request the release of the identity of his or her birth parents and their most current address shown in the records of the department or licensed adoption agency if the birth parent or parents have indicated consent to the disclosure in writing.

The birth parent may request disclosure of the name and most current address of the adopted person if the adopted person is age 21 or older and has indicated in writing that he or she wishes his or her name and address to be disclosed.

The adoptive parent of an adopted person under age 21 may request disclosure of the identity of a birth parent and the birth parent's most current address shown in the records if the department or licensed adoption agency

14 Child Welfare Information Gateway

finds that a medical necessity or other extraordinary circumstances justify the disclosure.

If an adult adopted person and the birth parents have each filed a written consent with the department or licensed adoption agency, the department or agency may arrange for contact between those persons.

Information about a birth sibling may be released to another sibling provided both are age 21 or older and have provided a written waiver.

Photos, letters, and other personal property may be released upon request if the adopted person is age 18 or older and other conditions have been met.

Access to Original Birth Certificate
Citation: Health & Safety Code § 102705
The original birth certificate is available only by order of the court.

Where the Information Can Be Located

- California Department of Social Services
- The licensed agency involved in the adoption

Colorado

Who May Access Information
Citation: Rev. Stat. §§ 19-5-304(1)(b); 19-5-305(2)(b)(I)
A qualified confidential intermediary is authorized to inspect confidential relinquishment and adoption records, postadoption records, and dependency and neglect records, including but not limited to court files, for the purpose of arranging contact, within 45 days after a motion to the court is filed by the following persons:

- An adult adopted person
- An adoptive parent, custodial grandparent, or legal guardian of a minor adopted person
- A biological parent or an adult biological sibling or half-sibling of an adult adopted person
- An adult descendant, spouse of an adopted person, adult stepchild, or adopted adult sibling of an adopted person with the notarized written consent of the adult adopted person
- A biological grandparent of an adopted with the notarized written consent of the biological parent (no written consent required if the biological parent is deceased)

Access to Adoption Records

- The legal representative of any of the individuals listed above
- A former foster child who may or may not have been adopted, who is age 18 or older, and who is searching for a birth sibling who also is age 18 or older, who may or may not have been adopted, and who may or may not have been in the foster care system

Upon request, the custodian of records shall provide direct access, without redaction, to all adoption records for inspection and copying by an adult adopted person, an adoptive parent of a minor adopted person, a custodial grandparent of a minor adopted person, or the legal representative of any such individual. In addition, the custodian of records shall provide direct access to adoption records for inspection and copying by a spouse, an adult descendant, an adult sibling or half-sibling, an adoptive parent or grandparent of an adult adopted person, or the legal representative of any such individual, if the individual requesting access has the notarized written consent of the adult adopted person or if the adopted person is deceased.

Access to Nonidentifying Information
Citation: Rev. Stat. §§ 19-5-402; 19-1-103(80)
Any adult adopted person or any adoptive parent may request nonidentifying information about the adopted person or the birth parents of the adopted person from the Department of Human Services. The department shall provide the nonidentifying information that is available to the department directly to the inquiring adult adopted person, adoptive parent, or to a qualified, licensed child-placing agency.

The term 'nonidentifying information' means information that does not disclose the name, address, place of employment, or any other material information that would lead to the identification of the birth parents, including, but not limited to, the following:

- The physical description of the birth parents
- The educational background of the birth parents
- The occupation of the birth parents
- Genetic information about the birth family
- Medical information about the adult adopted person's birth
- Social information about the birth parents
- The placement history of the adopted person

Mutual Access to Identifying Information
Citation: Rev. Stat. §§ 19-5-304; 19-5-305; 19-1-103(6.5)(a.5)

An eligible person may petition the court to appoint a confidential intermediary to search adoption records in an effort to find a birth relative. When a sought-after birth relative is located, the intermediary shall obtain consent from both parties that they wish to personally communicate with one another. Contact shall be made between the parties involved in the investigation only when consent for such contact has been received by the court.

All confidential intermediaries shall inform both the requesting birth relative and the sought-after birth relative of the existence of the voluntary adoption registry set forth in § 25-2-113.5.

The State registrar shall provide a birth parent with a contact preference form on which the birth parent may indicate a preference regarding contact by the adult adopted person or the adopted person's descendant. The form may include an updated medical history about the birth parent or other biological relatives. The State registrar shall maintain the contact preference form and themedical history statements, if any, and make them accessible to a person who is eligible to receive adoption records.

The 'adoption record' includes the following documents and information, without redaction:

- The adopted person's original birth certificate and amended birth certificate
- The final decree of adoption
- Any identifying information, including:
  - The name of the adopted person before placement for adoption
  - The name and address of each birth parent as they appear in the birth records
  - The name, address, and any contact information of the adult adopted person
  - The current name, address, and contact information of each birth parent, if known
  - Other information that might personally identify a birth parent
- Any nonidentifying information

Access to Adoption Records

Access to Original Birth Certificate
Citation: Rev. Stat. § 19-5-305

The option on the contact preference form that allows a birth parent to authorize or not authorize the release of the original birth certificate to eligible parties expires on January 1, 2016. On and after January 1, 2016, contact preference forms shall only address a birth parent's preferences regarding contact and to submit or update medical history. On and after July 1, 2014, the State registrar shall post a notice on its website stating that the contact preference form will be revised to eliminate that option and that birth parents may exercise this option prior to January 1, 2016.

Prior to allowing access to an original birth certificate, the State registrar must search for a contact preference form executed prior to January 1, 2016 to ascertain if either birth parent had stated a preference authorizing or not authorizing the release of the original birth certificate. If both birth parents have filed a contact preference form executed prior to January 1, 2016, authorizing the release of the original birth certificate, then the State registrar must release the original birth certificate to the eligible party. If there is no contact preference form on file, or if a contact preference form executed prior to January 1, 2016, is on file stating that the original birth certificate not be released, then the State registrar may not release the original birth certificate prior to January 1, 2016, unless the birth parent rescinds the contact preference form, upon mutual consent of two or more reunited parties, the birth parent is deceased, or the eligible party obtains a court order pursuant to § 19-1-309. When one birth parent has authorized the release of the birth certificate and the other birth parent has filed a contact preference form, prior to January 1, 2016, not authorizing release, the State registrar shall issue the original birth certificate to the eligible party with the name of the nonconsenting parent redacted.

Where the Information Can Be Located

- Colorado Department of Public Health and Environment
- Colorado Intermediary Services
- The child-placing agency involved in the adoption

Connecticut

Who May Access Information
Citation: Ann. Stat. § 45a-746
Nonidentifying information is available to the following persons:

- The adult adopted person
- The adoptive parents or guardian of the child
- The legal representative of the adopted person
- If the adopted person is deceased, any adult descendants, including adopted descendants

Identifying information may be accessed by:

- The adult adopted person
- Any birth parent of the adult adopted person, including any person claiming to be the father who was not a party to the proceedings for the termination of parental rights
- Any adult birth sibling of the adult adopted person
- If the adopted person is deceased, any adult descendants, including legally adopted descendants

Access to Nonidentifying Information
Citation: Ann. Stat. § 45a-746
Nonidentifying information about the birth parents shall be provided in writing to the adopting parents prior to finalization of the adoption.

The birth parents may access the information at any time for the purposes of verifying, correcting, or adding information. Information about the birth parents includes, but is not limited to:

- Age at the time of the child's birth
- Ethnic background and nationality
- General physical appearance at the time of the child's birth
- Education and occupations of the birth parents
- Talents, hobbies, and special interests
- Existence of any other children born to either parent
- Health history of the birth parents and blood relatives

Access to Adoption Records

- Reasons for placing the child for adoption
- Religion of the birth parents
- Any other relevant nonidentifying information

Mutual Access to Identifying Information
Citation: Ann. Stat. § 45a-751

Any authorized applicant may, by applying in person or in writing to the child-placing agency or the department, request the release of identifying information. The information should be released unless:

- The consents of every person whose identity is sought, as required by § 45a-751b, are not given.
- The release of the requested information would seriously disrupt or endanger the physical or emotional health of the applicant or the person whose identity is being requested.

Access to Original Birth Certificate
Citation: Ann. Stat. § 7-53

Upon request, the Department of Public Health shall issue an uncertified copy of an original certificate of birth to:

- An adopted person who is age 18 or older whose adoption was finalized on or after October 1, 1983
- An adopted person's adult child or grandchild

The certificate shall be marked with a notation by the issuer that the original certificate of birth has been superseded by a replacement certificate of birth as on file. Additionally, a notice shall be printed on such certificate or attached thereto stating that information related to the birth parents' preferences regarding contact by the adopted person or the adopted person's adult child or grandchild and a medical health history form completed by the birth parent may be on file with the Department of Children and Families.

Where the Information Can Be Located

- Connecticut Department of Children and Families
- The department and each child-placing agency involved in the adoption

Delaware

Who May Access Information
Citation: Ann. Code Tit. 13, § 924

Family information may be available to the following persons:

- The adopted person who is age 21 or older
- All other parties to an adoption

Access to Nonidentifying Information
Citation: Ann. Code Tit. 13, § 924

The department or agency may release nonidentifying information in its records to the parties to the adoption.

Mutual Access to Identifying Information
Citation: Ann. Code Tit. 13, §§ 924; 929; 962

Identifying information shall not be released except by order of the court or with the consent of all parties when it is deemed by the agency to be in the adopted person's best interests. In cases where the adopted person's health or the health of any blood relative is concerned and the adoption agency has refused to release the health information, the court may, through petition by the adopted person, permit the party to inspect only that part of the adoption agency or court record containing medical information if it is needed for the health of the person or of any blood relative of the person.

As part of the adoption planning process, the department or agency may provide information to the birth parents and to the adoptive parents as follows:

- In preplacement planning, identifying information shall be limited to the viewing of photographs, provided that such viewing is with the consent of birth parents and adoptive parents and that no additional identifying information is contained in the photographs.
- After a placement has been completed, and prior to finalization of the adoption, identifying information may include, but is not limited to, the exchange of names, addresses, photographs, and face-to-face meetings, provided that:
  - The birth parents and adoptive parents request the exchange of information in writing.
  - The birth parents, adoptive parents, and the department or agency agree to the exchange of information as specified in writing.

Access to Adoption Records

- The birth parents and adoptive parents acknowledge in writing their understanding that no legal right or assurance of continuing contact after finalization of the adoption exists.

An adopted person who is age 21 or older may request an agency to assist in locating a birth relative. When the relative is located, he or she may make a no-contact declaration. If the declaration is not made, the agency may release the birth parent or sibling's current name, address, and telephone number to the adopted person.

Access to Original Birth Certificate
Citation: Ann. Code Tit. 13, § 923
An adopted person who is age 21 or older may request a copy of the original birth certificate unless the birth parent has filed an affidavit denying release of identifying information.
Where the Information Can Be Located

- Delaware Office of Vital Statistics
- The agency involved in the adoption

District of Columbia

Who May Access Information
This issue is not addressed in the statutes reviewed.
Access to Nonidentifying Information
This issue is not addressed in the statutes reviewed.
Mutual Access to Identifying Information
Citation: Ann. Code § 16-311
All records are sealed and may not be inspected except upon order of the court, and then only if the welfare of the child is promoted.
Access to Original Birth Certificate
Citation: Ann. Code § 16-314
The original birth certificate is a sealed record that cannot be opened without order of the court.
Where the Information Can Be Located

- District of Columbia Child and Family Services Agency
- The agency involved in the adoption

Florida

Who May Access Information
Citation: Ann. Stat. §§ 63.162; 63.165
Information may be available to:

- The adopted person who is age 18 or older
- The birth parents
- The adoptive parents
- Birth siblings
- Maternal and paternal birth grandparents

Access to Nonidentifying Information
Citation: Ann. Stat. § 63.162
All nonidentifying information, including the family medical history and social history of the adopted person and the birth parents, when available, must be furnished to the adoptive parents before the adoption becomes final and to the adopted person, upon the adopted person's request, after he or she reaches majority. Upon the request of the adoptive parents, all nonidentifying information obtained before or after the adoption has become final must be furnished to the adoptive parents.

Mutual Access to Identifying Information
Citation: Ann. Stat. §§ 63.162; 63.165
Identifying information about a birth parent, an adoptive parent, or an adopted person may not be disclosed unless the respective party has authorized in writing the release of such information. If the adopted person is younger than age 18, written consent must be obtained from an adoptive parent.

The court may, upon petition of an adult adopted person or birth parent, for good cause shown, appoint an intermediary or a licensed child-placing agency to contact a birth parent or adult adopted person, as applicable, who has not registered with the adoption registry pursuant to § 63.165, and advise of both the availability of the intermediary or agency and that the birth parent or adult adopted person, as applicable, wishes to establish contact.

The department shall maintain a registry with the last known names and addresses of an adopted person, the birth parents, and the adoptive parents and any other identifying information that the parties wish to include in the registry.

The registry shall be available for those persons choosing to enter information therein, but no one shall be required to do so. A person who enters information in the registry must indicate clearly the persons to whom he or she is consenting to release the information, and shall be limited to the adopted person, the birth parents, the adoptive parents, birth siblings, and maternal and paternal birth grandparents. Consent to the release of this information may be made in the case of a minor adopted person by his or her adoptive parents or by the court after a showing of good cause. At any time, any person may withdraw, limit, or otherwise restrict consent to release information by notifying the department in writing.

Access to Original Birth Certificate
Citation: Ann. Stat. § 63.162
The original birth certificate is available only upon order of the court.

Where the Information Can Be Located
Florida Adoption Reunion Registry, Florida Department of Children and Families

Georgia

Who May Access Information
Citation: Ann. Code § 19-8-23
Information may be accessed by:

- The adult adopted person
- The birth parents
- Adult birth siblings
- The child of the adopted person, if the adopted person is deceased
- The adoptive parents

The adoptive parents may access only nonidentifying information.

Access to Nonidentifying Information
Citation: Ann. Code § 19-8-23
When certain information would assist in the provision of medical care, a medical emergency, or medical diagnosis or treatment, a party to the adoption; child; legal guardian; health-care agent of an adopted person; or a provider of medical services to a party to the adoption, child, legal guardian, or health-care agent may request that the department or child-placing agency access its own records on finalized adoptions for the purpose of adding subsequently obtained medical information or releasing nonidentifying medical and health history

24 Child Welfare Information Gateway

information contained in its records pertaining to an adopted person, the biological parents, or relatives of the biological parents of the adopted person.

When the State Adoption Unit of the Division of Family and Children Services or a child-placing agency receives documented medical information relevant to an adopted person, the office or child-placing agency shall use reasonable efforts to contact the adoptive parents of the adopted person if the adopted person is younger than age 18, or the adopted person if he or she is age 18 or older, and provide the documented medical information to the adoptive parents or the adopted person.

Upon the written request of an adopted person age 18 or older or an adoptive parent on behalf of an adopted person, nonidentifying information shall be released regarding the birth parents and the adopted person's birth, including the date and place of the adopted person's birth and the genetic, social, and health history of the birth parents.

Mutual Access to Identifying Information
Citation: Ann. Code § 19-8-23

Upon written request of an adopted person age 21 or older, the name of the birth parents shall be released if the birth parent has submitted an unrevoked written consent. If a birth parent has not filed an unrevoked written consent, the department shall, within 6 months of receipt of the written request, make a diligent effort to notify each birth parent, by personal and confidential contact, that a request for information has been made. The birth parent may then file an affidavit consenting or objecting to disclosure.

The adopted person also may petition the court to seek the release of information. The court shall grant the petition if it finds that failure to release the identity of each parent would have an adverse impact upon the physical, mental, or emotional health of the adopted person.

Birth parents and adult birth siblings also may access information about an adopted person using the same procedure. If the adopted person is deceased and leaves a child, such child, upon reaching age 21, may seek the name and other identifying information concerning his or her grandparents in the same manner as the deceased adopted person and subject to the same procedures.

The Office of Adoptions within the department shall maintain a registry for the recording of requests by adopted persons for the name of any birth parent, the written consent or the written objections of any birth parent to the release of that parent's identity to an adopted person, and for nonidentifying information regarding any birth parent.

Access to Adoption Records 25

Access to Original Birth Certificate
Citation: Ann. Code § 31-10-14
The original birth certificate is accessible only by order of the court or as provided by statute.
Where the Information Can Be Located
Georgia Adoption Reunion Registry

Guam

Who May Access Information
Citation: Ann. Code Tit. 19, § 4217
Adoption records are accessible only to persons or agencies that have a legitimate interest in the adoption.
Access to Nonidentifying Information
Citation: Ann. Code Tit. 19, § 4217
Social records may be furnished to persons and agencies having a legitimate interest in the protection, welfare, and treatment of the child or in research studies, in such manner as the court determines. Social records include the social service records, social studies, reports and related papers, and correspondence, including medical, psychological, and psychiatric studies and reports, either in the possession of the court or the division.
Mutual Access to Identifying Information
Citation: Ann. Code Tit. 19, § 4217
Access to information from the adoption record is available through court order only.
Access to Original Birth Certificate
Citation: Ann. Code Tit. 10, § 3215
The original birth certificate is accessible only upon order of the court.
Where the Information Can Be Located
The court that approved the adoption

Hawaii

Who May Access Information
Citation: Rev. Stat. §§ 578-14.5; 578-15
Health information may be provided to:

26 Child Welfare Information Gateway

- The adult adopted person
- The adoptive parent
- The minor adopted person's guardian or custodian

Adoption records may be accessed by:

- The adult adopted person
- The adoptive parents
- The birth parents

Access to Nonidentifying Information
Citation: Rev. Stat. §§ 578-14.5; 578-15

The Department of Health shall prepare a standard medical information form to obtain medical information on the birth parents of the minor adopted person. This form shall include a request for any information about the adopted child's potential genetic or other inheritable diseases, including similar medical histories, if known, of the parents of the birth parents. All child-placing organizations shall make reasonable efforts to complete this form on both birth parents, to obtain from the natural parents written consent to the release of this information to or for the benefit of the adopted child, and whenever possible, to obtain from the natural mother a signed release to receive a copy of all of her medical records relating to the birth of the adopted child that are in the possession of the hospital or other facility at which the child was born. The completed forms shall be included in the department's adoption records.

Upon written application from the adult adopted person; or the adoptive parent, guardian, or custodian on behalf of a minor adopted person; the Department of Health shall furnish the applicant with a copy of the completed forms. The department is authorized to disclose the information without prior court approval.

Information concerning the ethnic background and necessary medical information may be released regardless of the presence of a confidentiality affidavit.

Mutual Access to Identifying Information
Citation: Rev. Stat. § 578-15

An adopted person who is age 18 or older may submit a written request to the family court for inspection of adoption records. Such records will be released unless the birth parents have filed a confidentiality affidavit. Such affidavits may be renewed every 10 years. The adopted person may submit an affidavit consenting to the inspection of records by the birth parents.

Access to Original Birth Certificate
Citation: Rev. Stat. §§ 578-14; 578-15; 338-20
If a new birth certificate is issued, the original birth certificate shall be sealed. The sealed document may be opened by the department only by an order of a court or when requested in accordance with § 578-15.

The birth parent may be provided a copy of the original birth certificate upon request.

Where the Information Can Be Located
Family Court Central Registry

Idaho

Who May Access Information
Citation: Ann. Code § 39-259A
Identifying information may be made available to:

- The adult adopted person
- The birth parents
- Adult birth siblings

Access to Nonidentifying Information
Citation: Ann. Code § 16-1506
A copy of all medical and genetic information compiled as part of the adoption investigation shall be made available to the adopting family by the department or other investigating children's adoption agency prior to entry of the final order of adoption.

Mutual Access to Identifying Information
Citation: Ann. Code § 39-259A
The State Registrar of Vital Statistics shall establish and maintain a confidential list of qualified adult adopted persons, birth parents, or adult birth siblings who have consented to the release of their identifying information. Any consent shall indicate the person's desired method of notification in the event that a match occurs, and shall also indicate whether the applicant desires the release of identifying information if a match occurs after his or her death.

28   Child Welfare Information Gateway

The applicant may revise his or her consent with respect to change of address or method of notification.

A birth parent shall not be matched with an adult adopted person without the consent of the other birth parent unless:

- There is only one birth parent listed on the birth certificate.
- The other birth parent is deceased.
- The other birth parent cannot be found by the Department of Health and Welfare or by a licensed child-placing agency.

Access to Original Birth Certificate
Citation: Ann. Code § 39-258
The original birth certificate is available upon a court order or, in accordance with § 39-259A, when all parties have consented through the State adoption registry.
Where the Information Can Be Located
Idaho Voluntary Adoption Registry, Vital Records Section, Bureau of Vital Records and Health Statistics

Illinois

Who May Access Information
Citation: Comp. Stat. Ch. 750, §§ 50/18.1; 50/18.4
The following persons may apply to the Illinois Adoption Registry:

- Either birth parent
- If the birth parent is deceased, the adopted person's adult birth sibling, birth aunt, or birth uncle
- Any adult adopted person or any adoptive parent or legal guardian of an adopted person under age 21
- If the adopted person is deceased, any surviving spouse, adult child, or adult grandchild
- Any adoptive parent or legal guardian of a deceased adult adopted person

The services of a confidential intermediary may be utilized by the following persons:

Access to Adoption Records

29

- Any adopted person age 21 or older
- Any adoptive parent or legal guardian of an adopted person under age 21
- Any birth parent of an adopted person who is age 21 or older
- Any adult child or adult grandchild of a deceased adopted person
- Any adoptive parent or surviving spouse of a deceased adopted person
- Any adult birth sibling of the adult adopted person, unless the birth parent has checked Option E on the Birth Parent Preference Form or has filed a Denial of Information Exchange with the Adoption Registry and is not deceased
- Any adult adopted birth sibling of an adult adopted person
- Any adult birth sibling of the birth parent if the birth parent is deceased

Nonidentifying information may be provided to the adoptive parents, the adopted person, or legal guardian who is a registrant of the Illinois Adoption Registry.

Access to Nonidentifying Information
Citation: Comp. Stat. Ch. 750, § 50/18.4
The adoptive parents shall receive in writing the following nonidentifying information, if known, not later than the date of placement of the child:

- The birth parents' age
- The birth parents' race, religion, and ethnic background
- The general physical appearance of the birth parents
- The birth parents' education, occupation, hobbies, interests, and talents
- The existence of any other children born to the birth parents
- Information about birth grandparents, their reason for emigrating into the United States, if applicable, and country of origin
- The relationship between the birth parents
- Detailed medical and mental health histories of the child, the birth parents, and their immediate relatives
- The actual date and place of birth of the adopted person

No information provided under this subsection shall disclose the name or last known address of the birth parents, grandparents, the siblings of the birth parents, the adopted person, or any other relative of the adopted person.

Child Welfare Information Gateway

Any adopted person age 18 or older shall be given the information listed above upon request.

The Illinois Adoption Registry shall release any of the nonidentifying information above that appears on the certified copy of the original birth certificate or the Certificate of Adoption to an adopted person, adoptive parent, or legal guardian who is a registrant of the Illinois Adoption Registry.

Mutual Access to Identifying Information
Citation: Comp. Stat. Ch. 750, §§ 50/18.1; 50/18.3a

The Department of Public Health shall establish and maintain a registry for the purpose of allowing mutually consenting members of birth and adoptive families to exchange identifying and medical information. Identifying information includes any one or more of the following:

- The name and last known address of the consenting person or persons
- A copy of the Illinois Adoption Registry Application of the consenting person or persons
- A noncertified copy of the original birth certificate of an adult adopted person

Written authorization from all parties identified must be received prior to disclosure of any identifying information, with the exception of noncertified copies of original birth certificates released to adult adopted persons or to surviving adult children and spouses of deceased adopted persons.

At any time after a child is surrendered for adoption, any time during the adoption proceedings, or at any time thereafter, either birth parent or both of them may file with the registry a birth parent registration identification form.

The department shall supply identifying information to the adopted person or his or her adoptive parents, legal guardians, adult children, adult grandchildren, or surviving spouse, and to a birth aunt or uncle only if both the adopted person and one of his or her eligible relatives have filed with the registry an information exchange authorization.

Any person listed above may petition the court for the appointment of a confidential intermediary for the purpose of exchanging medical information, obtaining identifying information, or arranging contact with one or more mutually consenting biological relatives. The petitioner shall be required to accompany his or her petition with proof of registration with the Illinois Adoption Registry and Medical Information Exchange.

Access to Original Birth Certificate
Citation: Comp. Stat. Ch. 750, § 50/18.1b

Any adopted person who was born in Illinois prior to January 1, 1946, may file with the Illinois Adoption Registry a request for a noncertified copy of an original birth certificate. The registry shall provide the adopted person with an unaltered, noncertified copy of his or her original birth certificate upon receipt of the request. In cases in which an adopted person born prior to January 1, 1946, is deceased, and one of his or her surviving adult children, adult grandchildren, or spouse has registered with the registry, he or she may complete and file with the registry a request for a copy of the birth certificate. The registry shall provide such surviving adult child, adult grandchild, or spouse with an unaltered, noncertified copy of the adopted person's original birth certificate upon receipt of the request.

Beginning November 15, 2011, any adult adopted person who was born in Illinois on or after January 1, 1946, may file with the registry a request for a noncertified copy of an original birth certificate. In cases in which the adopted person is deceased, his or her surviving adult child, adult grandchild, or spouse who has registered with the registry may request a noncertified copy of the original birth certificate.

If the registry confirms that a requesting adult adopted person, the parent of a requesting adult child of a deceased adopted person, or the husband or wife of a requesting surviving spouse was not the object of a Denial of Information Exchange filed by a birth parent on or before January 1, 2011, and that no birth parent named on the original birth certificate has filed a Birth Parent Preference Form where Option E (prohibiting the release of identifying information) was selected prior to the receipt of a request for an original birth certificate, the registry shall provide the adult adopted person or his or her surviving adult child or spouse with an unaltered noncertified copy of the adopted person's original birth certificate.

Where the Information Can Be Located

- Illinois Adoption Registry, Illinois Department of Public Health
- Confidential Intermediary Service of Illinois, Midwest Adoption Center (MAC)

Indiana

Who May Access Information
Citation: Ann. Stat. § 31-19-22-2
The following persons may request the release of identifying information:

- An adult adopted person
- A birth parent
- An adoptive parent
- The spouse or relative of a deceased adopted person
- The spouse or relative of a deceased birth parent

Access to Nonidentifying Information
Citation: Ann. Stat. §§ 31-19-17-3; 31-19-17-5
The person, licensed child-placing agency, or county office shall release all available social, medical, psychological, and educational records concerning the child to:

- The prospective adoptive parent or adoptive parent
- Upon request, the adopted person who is at least age 21 and provides proof of identification

The report shall exclude information that would identify the birth parents unless the adoptive parent, prospective adoptive parent, or adopted person who requests the information knows the identity of the birth parents.

For an adoption that was granted before July 1, 1993: Upon the request of an adopted person who is at least age 21, the licensed child-placing agency or a county office shall provide to the adopted person available information from social, medical, psychological, and educational records and reports. Information that would identify the birth parents shall be excluded from the report unless an adopted person already knows the identity of the birth parents.

Mutual Access to Identifying Information
Citation: Ann. Stat. §§ 31-19-22-2; 31-19-25-2; 31-19-25-2.5; 31-19-25-3
Identifying information may not be released unless the adult adopted person and the birth parent have submitted a written consent to the State Registrar or the person from whom the identifying information is requested

Access to Adoption Records

that allows the release of the information to the individual requesting the information.

Identifying information for an adopted person who is younger than age 21 may not be released unless the adopted person's adoptive parent has submitted a written consent for the release of identifying information.

For adoptions after December 31, 1993: Identifying information shall be released only if the adopted person has submitted a written consent to the State Registrar or the person who has requested the release of identifying information. If the adopted person is younger than age 21, identifying information may not be released unless the adopted person's adoptive parent has submitted a written consent for the release of identifying information.

A birth parent may restrict access to his or her identifying information by filing a written nonrelease form with the State Registrar. The nonrelease form:

- Remains in effect during the period indicated by the individual submitting the form
- Is renewable
- May be withdrawn at any time by the individual who submitted the form

The nonrelease form is no longer in effect if the birth parent consents in writing to the release of identifying information and has not withdrawn that consent. A nonrelease form is no longer in effect if the birth parent who filed the nonrelease form is deceased, unless the nonrelease form specifically states that the nonrelease form remains in effect after the birth parent's death.

Access to Original Birth Certificate
Citation: Ann. Stat. § 31-19-13-2
The original birth certificate is withheld from inspection except for a child adopted by a stepparent or as provided in statutes pertaining to release of identifying information.

Where the Information Can Be Located
Indiana Adoption History Registry, Indiana State Department of Health, Vital Statistics

Iowa

Who May Access Information
Citation: Ann. Stat. § 144.43A
The following persons may register with the mutual consent voluntary adoption registry:

- The adult adopted person
- An adult sibling
- The birth parents

Access to Nonidentifying Information
Citation: Ann. Stat. § 600.16
Any information compiled relating to medical history, developmental history, and social history of the person to be adopted shall be made available at any time by the clerk of court, the department, or any agency that made the placement to:

- The adopting parents
- The adopted person who is age 21 or older
- Any person approved by the department if the person uses this information solely for the purposes of conducting a legitimate medical research project or of treating a patient in a medical facility
- A descendant of an adopted person

The identity of the adopted person's birth parents shall not be disclosed.

Mutual Access to Identifying Information
Citation: Ann. Stat. § 144.43A
The State Registrar shall reveal the identity of the birth parent to the adult adopted person or the identity of the adult adopted person to the birth parent, shall notify the parties that the requests have been matched, and shall disclose the identifying information to those parties if all of the following conditions are met:

- A birth parent has filed a request and provided consent to the disclosure of his or her identity to the adult adopted person upon request of the adult adopted person.
- An adult adopted person has filed a request and provided consent to the disclosure of his or her identity to a birth parent upon request of the birth parent.

Access to Adoption Records

- The State Registrar has been provided sufficient information to make the requested match.

If the adult adopted person has a sibling who is a minor and who also has been adopted, the request will be denied.

The State Registrar shall reveal the identity of the adult adopted person to an adult sibling if the following conditions are met:

- An adult adopted person has filed a request and provided consent to the disclosure of his or her identity to an adult sibling.
- The adult sibling has filed a request and provided consent to the revelation of his or her identity to the adult adopted person.
- The State Registrar has been provided with sufficient information to make the requested match.

A person who has filed a request or provided consent may withdraw the consent at any time prior to the release of any information by filing a written withdrawal-of-consent statement with the State Registrar. The adult adopted person, adult sibling, and birth parent shall notify the State Registrar of any change in the information contained in a filed request or consent.

Access to Original Birth Certificate
Citation: Ann. Stat. § 144.24

The original birth certificate may not be inspected except under order of a court. The State Registrar shall, upon the application of an adult adopted person, a birth parent, an adoptive parent, or the legal representative of the any of the former, inspect the original birth certificate and reveal to the applicant the date of the adoption and the name and address of the court that issued the adoption decree.

Where the Information Can Be Located

Iowa Mutual Consent Voluntary Adoption Registry, Iowa Department of Public Health, Bureau of Vital Records

Kansas

Who May Access Information
Citation: Ann. Stat. § 59-2122

The files and records of the court in adoption proceedings shall not be open to inspection or copy by persons other than the parties in interest and

36 Child Welfare Information Gateway

their attorneys, representatives of the State Department for Children and Families, and the Commission on Judicial Performance in the discharge of the commission's duties, except upon an order of the court expressly permitting the same. As used in this section, parties in interest shall not include genetic parents once a decree of adoption is entered.

Access to Nonidentifying Information
Citation: Ann. Stat. § 59-2122
The Department for Children and Families may contact the adoptive parents of the minor child or the adult adopted person at the request of the genetic parents in the event of a health or medical need. The department may contact the adult adopted person at the request of the genetic parents for any reason.

Mutual Access to Identifying Information
Citation: Ann. Stat. § 59-2122
Identifying information shall not be shared with the genetic parents without the permission of the adoptive parents of the minor child or the adult adopted person.

Access to Original Birth Certificate
Citation: Ann. Stat. § 65-2423
The original birth certificate is a sealed document that may be opened by the State Registrar only upon the demand of the adult adopted person or by an order of the court.

Where the Information Can Be Located
Kansas Department for Children and Family Services, Post Adoption Search and Records

Kentucky

Who May Access Information
Citation: Rev. Stat. §§ 199.520; 199.572; 199.575
Nonidentifying information may be provided to:

- The adopted person who is age 18 or older
- the individual requesting the information.

Identifying information is accessible to:

- The adopted person who is age 18 or older

Access to Adoption Records   37

- A birth sibling who is age 18 or older
- A birth parent

Access to Nonidentifying Information
Citation: Rev. Stat. § 199.520

The health history and other nonidentifying background information of the birth parents and blood relatives of the adopted person shall be given to the adoptive parents and the court no later than the date of finalization of the adoption proceedings.

The information shall be made available upon the request, in person or in writing, of the adult adopted person. The information shall not be made available if it is of a nature that would tend to identify the birth parents of the adopted person, except as provided in §§ 199.570 and 199.572.

Mutual Access to Identifying Information
Citation: Rev. Stat. §§ 199.572; 199.575

If the birth parents have given consent, the adult adopted person may inspect the records pertaining to his or her adoption proceedings upon written request. If the birth parents have not given consent, the Cabinet for Health and Family Services may notify the birth parents that the adult adopted person has made a request for information. The notification shall be by personal and confidential contact, without disclosing the identity of the adult adopted person.

If, after a diligent effort, the secretary of the cabinet certifies that both birth parents identified in the original birth certificate are deceased or is unable to locate the parents, then a judge may order that all adoption records shall be open for inspection to the adult adopted person. In any case, the court shall order that only identifying information about the birth parents be shared with the adult adopted person.

In situations where a preadoptive brother or sister relationship existed, and one or more of these siblings was then adopted, the following procedures shall be followed on an inquiry by one or more of the siblings to the cabinet seeking information about his brother or sister:

- In all cases, an adopted person age 18 or older or a preadoptive sibling age 18 or older may file information with the cabinet about himself or herself, his or her present location, and his or her known antecedents, stating his or her interest in being reunited with his or her preadoptive siblings and authorizing the cabinet to release such information to any preadoptive siblings who may make similar inquiry.

38   Child Welfare Information Gateway

- In any case in which a person age 18 or older requests information about or expresses a desire in being reunited with a preadoptive sibling, the cabinet shall first determine whether the sibling has made similar inquiry. If the sibling has previously authorized release of information, the cabinet shall release the information to the sibling making inquiry.

Access to Original Birth Certificate
Citation: Rev. Stat. § 199.570
The original birth certificate is available only upon court order.
Where the Information Can Be Located
Kentucky Cabinet for Families and Children

Louisiana

Who May Access Information
Citation: Ch. Code Art. 1126; 1270
The voluntary adoption registry may be used by:

- The adopted person who is at least age 18
- The birth mother and birth father
- The parents or siblings of a deceased birth parent
- An adoptive parent of a minor or deceased adopted person
- The birth siblings who are age 18 or older

Nonidentifying information shall be provided to:

- The adoptive parents
- The adopted person who is age 18 or older
- The birth parents

Access to Nonidentifying Information
Citation: Ch. Code Art. 1126; 1127; 1127.1
The agency or person to whom a surrender is made shall have the duty to make a good faith effort to obtain the Statement of Family History required by Articles 1124 and 1125, to deliver it to prospective adoptive parents upon placement, and to make it available, upon request, to the adopted person at age 18 or older. If the Statement of Family History is subsequently transferred to

Access to Adoption Records

39

another agency or person, the new custodian of the information assumes responsibility to the adopted person.

Any adopted person (or his or her legal representative if the adopted person is still a minor) or a birth parent, may, upon written request, obtain nonidentifying medical or genetic information without the necessity of filing a motion for disclosure. Upon such a request, the agency or person shall make a good faith effort to review and abstract nonidentifying genetic or medical information from all available records and sources that are similar in content to the Statement of Family History.

After adoptive placement of the child, the agency or person to whom a surrender is made shall have a continuing duty to maintain these records and supplement them if additional nonidentifying medical or genetic information is received about the adopted child or a birth parent. Upon such a request, the agency or person shall disclose such information. In fulfilling this continuing duty, the agency or person is authorized to contact the adopted person, adoptive parents, and birth parents to provide updated nonidentifying medical and genetic information or to facilitate the exchange of information between the parties.

Mutual Access to Identifying Information
Citation: Ch. Code Art. 1270

The Office of Community Services of the Department of Social Services shall maintain a voluntary registry for the matching of adopted persons and birth parents or siblings, or both. The purpose of this registry shall be to facilitate voluntary contact between the adopted person and the birth parents, siblings, or both.

The use of the registry shall be limited to the adopted person who is at least age 18, the birth mother, the birth father, parents or siblings of a deceased birth parent, an adoptive parent of a minor or deceased adopted person, and any birth sibling who is at least age 18. No registration by an adopted person shall be permitted until all birth siblings who were adopted by the same adoptive parents have reached age 18.

The registry shall not release any information from adoption records in violation of the privacy or confidentiality rights of a birth parent who has not authorized the release of any information.

The registry shall confirm for an adopted person the fact of his or her adoption and identify the court in which the adoption was finalized and the agency, firm, or lawyer facilitating the adoption when that information is known by the department. To receive this information, the adopted person

40 Child Welfare Information Gateway

shall be age 18 or older, submit the request in writing, and provide proof of identity.

Access to Original Birth Certificate
Citation: Rev. Stat. § 40:73
The original birth certificate is available:

- Upon court order to the adopted person, or if deceased, the adopted person's descendants, or the adoptive parent
- To the agency that was a party to the adoption upon court order after a showing of compelling reasons

Where the Information Can Be Located
Louisiana Voluntary Adoption Registry, Department of Children and Family Services

Maine

Who May Access Information
Citation: Rev. Stat. Tit. 22, § 2706-A; Tit. 18-A, § 9-310
The following persons may participate in the adoption registry:

- An adoptive parent or legal guardian if the adopted person is under age 18, deceased, or incapacitated
- A birth parent
- A birth sibling or half-sibling who is age 18 or older
- The legal guardian or custodian of a person under age 18 who is the sibling or half-sibling of an adopted person
- If a birth parent is deceased, a birth mother, legal father, grandparent, sibling, half-sibling, aunt, uncle, or first cousin of the deceased birth parent

Medical or genetic information shall be made available to:

- The adopted person upon reaching age 18
- The adopted person's descendants
- The adoptive parents or the child's legal guardian on petition of the court

Access to Adoption Records

Access to Nonidentifying Information
Citation: Rev. Stat. Tit. 18-A, § 9-310; Tit. 22, § 8205

The licensed child-placing agency shall obtain medical and genetic information on the birth parents and the child that shall include:

- A current medical, psychological, and developmental history of the child, including an account of the child's prenatal care, medical condition at birth, results of newborn screening, and any drug or medication taken by the child's birth mother during pregnancy
- Any subsequent medical, psychological, or psychiatric examination
- Any physical, sexual, or emotional abuse suffered by the child
- A record of any immunizations and health care received since birth
- Relevant information concerning the medical, psychological, and social history of the birth parents

Prior to the child being placed for adoption, the licensed child-placing agency shall provide the information described above to the adoptive parents.

Any medical or genetic information in the court records relating to an adoption must be made available to the adopted child upon reaching age 18 and to the adopted child's descendants, adoptive parents, or legal guardian on petition of the court.

Mutual Access to Identifying Information
Citation: Rev. Stat. Tit. 22, § 2706-A; 2766

The State Registrar shall maintain a file of the names and addresses of adopted persons and their adoptive and birth parents who have registered with the registry. At the time of registration, each registrant shall indicate the persons with whom contact is desired. A registrant may withdraw from the adoption registry at any time by submitting a written request. The Registrar shall notify each party of the name and address of the other party and of sources of counseling when a request for contact is made.

An adult adopted person may request the identity or his or her birth parents from the Registrar by submitting proof that the birth parents are deceased, an affidavit from a blood relative who is not a sibling and who is at least 10 years older than the adopted person verifying that the adopted person lived with the birth parents for 5 years, and a court order authorizing the Registrar to open the original birth certificate to verify the identity of the birth parents. Upon verification of the information, the Registrar will prepare a form identifying the birth parents. This form must be attached to the new birth certificate and provided to the adopted person.

The State Registrar shall provide upon request each birth parent a contact preference form and a medical history form. A birth parent shall fill out a medical history form if he or she fills out a contact preference form.

A birth parent also may complete a contact preference form on which he or she may state a preference regarding contact by an adopted person. The form must indicate whether the birth parent chooses contact, contact through an intermediary, or no contact. Completed contact preference and medical history forms shall be attached to the original birth certificate of the adopted person. A completed contact preference form and medical history form have the same level of confidentiality as the original birth certificate.

Access to Original Birth Certificate
Citation: Rev. Stat. Tit. 22, §§ 2765; 2768

The original certificate of birth is not subject to inspection except upon order of the court or pursuant to § 2768.

An adopted person, his or her attorney, or, if the adopted person is deceased, his or her descendants may obtain a copy of that person's original certificate of birth from the State Registrar of Vital Statistics.

The adopted person must be at least age 18 and have been born in this State. The adopted person must file a written application and provide appropriate proof of identification to the State Registrar.

Upon receipt of the written application and proof of identification and fulfillment of the requirements listed below, the State Registrar shall issue a noncertified copy of the unaltered original certificate of birth to the applicant.

The State Registrar may require a waiting period and impose a fee for the noncertified copy. The fees and waiting period imposed under this subsection must be identical to the fees and waiting period generally imposed on persons seeking their own birth certificates.

If a contact preference or medical history form has been completed and submitted to the State Registrar pursuant to § 2769, the State Registrar also must provide that information.

Where the Information Can Be Located

Maine State Adoption Reunion Registry, Office of Vital Records

Access to Adoption Records — 43

Maryland

Who May Access Information
Citation: Fam. Law §§ 5-4C-05; 5-356; 5-357

Only the following persons may register with the adoption registry for the exchange of identifying information:

- Birth parents and siblings
- An adopted person, age 21 or older, who does not have a birth sibling under the age of 21 with the same adoptive parents

Nonidentifying and medical information shall be available to:

- The adoptive parents
- The adopted person
- The birth parents

Access to Nonidentifying Information
Citation: Fam. Law §§ 5-356; 5-357; 5-358

A local department shall make reasonable efforts to compile and make available to a prospective adoptive parent a comprehensive medical and mental health history of the prospective adoptive child. On request of an adoptive parent, a local department shall make reasonable efforts to compile a pertinent medical and mental health history of each of the adoptive child's birth parents, if available to the local department, and to make that history available to the adoptive parent. A medical or mental health history may not contain identifying information about a parent or former parent.

On request of an adopted person, adoptive parent, or birth parent, a local department shall provide information in its adoption record on the adopted person. The records that are accessed may not contain any identifying information.

If, after a hearing on a petition of an adopted person or birth parent, a court is satisfied that the adopted person, a blood relative of the adopted person, or a birth parent urgently needs medical information not in department and court records, the court may appoint an intermediary to try to contact the adopted person or a birth parent for the information.

Mutual Access to Identifying Information
Citation: Fam. Law §§ 5-4C-06; 5-4C-07

Child Welfare Information Gateway

To register with the Registry, an individual shall submit a notarized affidavit containing identifying information, including the individual's current name, any previous name by which the individual was known, address, and telephone number. A registrant may withdraw at any time by submitting an affidavit.

On receipt of an affidavit, the administration shall:

- Attempt to match registrants or to provide matching information
- If a match is made, direct the child-placing agency or the local department to notify the registrants through a confidential contact

Access to Original Birth Certificate
Citation: Fam. Law §§ 5-359; 5-3A-42; 5-3B-29
For adoptions finalized on or after January 1, 2000:

- An adopted person who is at least age 21 may apply to the secretary for a copy of his or her original birth certificate.
- If an adopted person is at least age 21, a birth parent may apply to the secretary for a copy of the adopted person's original birth certificate.

A birth parent may file with the director a disclosure veto to bar disclosure of information about that parent in an accessible record. The birth parent may also cancel a disclosure veto and refile a disclosure veto at any time.

An adult adopted person may file a disclosure veto to bar disclosure of information about him or her in an accessible record. The adopted person may also cancel a disclosure veto and refile a disclosure veto at any time.

Except as provided below, the secretary shall give to each applicant who meets the requirements of this section a copy of each record that the applicant requested and that the secretary has on file.

Whenever a birth parent applies for a record, the secretary shall redact from the copy all information as to:

- The other birth parent if that parent has filed a disclosure veto
- The adopted person and each adoptive parent if the adopted person has filed a disclosure veto

Whenever an adopted person applies for a record, the secretary shall redact from the copy all information as to the birth parent if that parent has filed a disclosure veto.

Access to Adoption Records

Where the Information Can Be Located
Mutual Consent Voluntary Adoption Registry, Maryland Social Services Administration

Massachusetts

Who May Access Information
Citation: Ann. Laws Ch. 210, § 5D
Nonidentifying information may be provided to:

- The adopted person who is age 18 or older
- The adoptive parents
- The birth parents

Identifying information may be released to:

- The adopted person who is age 21 or older
- The adoptive parents
- The birth parents

Access to Nonidentifying Information
Citation: Ann. Laws Ch. 210, § 5D
A placement agency that holds records relating to an adopted person, the birth parents, or the adoptive parents shall:

- Release to the adopted person who is age 18 or older, upon his or her written request, information about his or her birth parents that does not identify the birth parents or their present or former locations
- Release to a birth parent of an adopted person, upon the birth parent's written request, information about the adopted person that does not reveal his or her identity after adoption or his or her present or former locations
- Release to an adoptive parent, if the adopted person is under age 18, upon the adoptive parent's written request, information about the adopted person and his or her birth parents that does not identify the birth parents or their present or former locations

The information shall include such nonidentifying information that the agency holds concerning the medical, ethnic, socioeconomic, and educational circumstances of the person. The agency, in its discretion, shall further release such nonidentifying information concerning the circumstances under which the adopted person became available for adoption as it deems to be in the best interest of the person so requesting.

Mutual Access to Identifying Information
Citation: Ann. Laws Ch. 210, § 5D

If a placement agency has received written permission from a birth parent to release the identity of the birth parent to the adopted person and the agency has received written permission from the adopted person, or written permission from the adoptive parents if the adopted person is under age 21, to release the identity after adoption of the adopted person to the birth parent, then the agency shall release the identity of the adopted person to the birth parent and the identity of the birth parent to the adopted person.

The placement agency shall:

- Release to the birth parent, upon the birth parent's written request, any personal data that it holds relating to the birth parent
- Release to an adoptive parent, upon his or her written request, any personal data that it holds relating to the adoptive parent

In making any disclosure of information, the agency shall remove personal identifiers relating to a third person. All other adoption records held by the placement agency shall be confidential and shall not be released.

Access to Original Birth Certificate
Citation: Ann. Laws Ch. 210, § 5C

All records concerning the adoption proceedings are available only upon court order.

Where the Information Can Be Located

Adoption Search Coordinator, Massachusetts Department of Social Services

Michigan

Who May Access Information
Citation: Comp. Laws § 710.68
Nonidentifying information may be provided to:

- The adult adopted person
- The adoptive parents
- Birth parents and adult birth siblings

Identifying information may accessed by the birth parent, adult adopted person, and an adult former sibling.

Access to Nonidentifying Information
Citation: Comp. Laws § 710.68; 710.27
Within 63 days of a written request, the following information must be provided:

- The date and place of the child's birth
- The health and genetic history of the child, including prenatal care, condition at birth, and any drug taken by the child's mother during pregnancy
- Any subsequent medical, psychological, psychiatric, or dental examination done when the child was under the jurisdiction of the court
- Any neglect or physical, sexual, or emotional abuse suffered by the child
- A record of any immunizations and health care the child received while in foster care
- The health and genetic history of the child's birth parents and other members of the child's family
- The findings of any medical, psychological, or psychiatric evaluation of each parent at the time of placement
- If a parent is deceased, the cause of and the age at death
- A description of the child and the child's family of origin, including:
    - The first name of the child at birth
    - The age and sex of birth siblings
    - The child's educational background and any special educational needs

48 Child Welfare Information Gateway

- The child's racial, ethnic, and religious background
- A general description of the child's parents
- The child's past and existing relationship with any relative, foster parent, or other individual or facility
- The levels of educational, occupational, professional, athletic, or artistic achievement of the child's family
- Hobbies, special interests, and school activities of the child's family
- The circumstances of any order terminating the parental rights of a parent for abuse, neglect, abandonment, or other mistreatment of the child
- Length of time between the termination of parental rights and adoptive placement and whether the termination was voluntary or court-ordered
- Any information necessary to determine the child's eligibility for State or Federal benefits, including financial, medical, or other assistance

Mutual Access to Identifying Information
Citation: Comp. Laws §§ 710.27a; 710.68

A birth parent or adult former sibling who knows the birth name of the adopted person may file with the central adoption registry a statement consenting to or denying the release of the identifying information about that parent. The statement may be filed, updated, or revoked at any time.

Within 63 days after a request for identifying information about an adult adopted person is received, a child-placing agency, court, or the Department of Human Services shall provide in writing to the birth parent or adult birth sibling requesting the information the adult adopted person's most recent name and address, if the adult adopted person has given written consent to release the information. If written consent is not on file, a confidential intermediary may be used to locate the adult adopted person.

Upon a written request for identifying information from an adult adopted person, including a request for the name and address of an adult birth sibling, the agency, court, or department shall submit a clearance request form to the central adoption registry. After receipt of a clearance reply form from the central adoption registry, the agency or department shall notify the adopted person in writing of the identifying information to which the adopted person is entitled, or, if the identifying information cannot be released, the reason why the information cannot be released.

Access to Adoption Records | 49

For adoptions finalized between May 28, 1945, and September 12, 1980, identifying information shall be released to the adult adopted person on each birth parent who has consented to the release, or both birth parents if both have consented or if one or both parents are deceased. For adoptions finalized before May 28, 1945 or after September 12, 1980, identifying information may be released to an adult adopted person, unless the birth parent has filed a statement currently in effect with the central adoption registry denying consent to have identifying information released.

Access to Original Birth Certificate
Citation: Comp. Laws § 333.2882
A copy of the original birth certificate may be provided to the adult adopted person upon request when accompanied by a copy of a central adoption registry clearance reply form or by court order.

Where the Information Can Be Located
Michigan Confidential Intermediary Program, Michigan Department of Human Services

Minnesota

Who May Access Information
Citation: Ann. Stat. §§ 259.83; 259.89
Nonidentifying information may be provided to:

- The adopted person who is age 19 or older
- The adoptive parent

Identifying information may be provided to:

- The adopted person who is age 19 or older
- The birth parents
- Adult genetic siblings, if disclosure does not violate the confidentiality of the birth parents or if they give consent

Access to Nonidentifying Information
Citation: Ann. Stat. § 259.83
For adoptions finalized on or after August 1, 1994, the adopted person, if age 19 or older, or the adoptive parent may receive the detailed medical and social history that was provided at the time of the adoption. In addition, the

adult adopted person or the adoptive parent may request the agency to contact the birth parents to request current nonidentifying social and medical history of the adopted person's birth family.

When the agency receives information about a medical or genetic condition that has affected or may affect the physical or mental health of genetically related persons, the agency shall make a diligent effort to contact those persons in order to transmit the health information.

Mutual Access to Identifying Information
Citation: Ann. Stat. §§ 259.83; 259.89

Agencies shall provide assistance and counseling services when the adoptive parents, birth parents, or adopted person who is age 19 or older request current information. The agency shall contact the other adult persons or the adoptive parents of a minor child in a personal and confidential manner to determine whether there is a desire to share information or to have contact. The agency shall provide services to adult genetic siblings if there is no known violation of the confidentiality of a birth parent or if the birth parent gives written consent. The adopted person also must be advised of other siblings who were adopted or relinquished to the commissioner but not adopted.

In adoptive placements made on and after August 1, 1982, the agency shall obtain from the birth parents an affidavit attesting that:

- The birth parent has been informed of the right of the adopted person at age 19 to request the name, last known address, birth date, and birthplace of the birth parents named on the original birth record.
- Each birth parent may file an affidavit objecting to the release of information about that birth parent, and that parent only, to the adopted person.
- If the birth parent does not file an affidavit objecting to release of information before the adopted person reaches age 19, the information will be released upon request.
- Notwithstanding the filing of an affidavit, the adopted person may petition the court for release of identifying information about a birth parent.
- The birth parent shall then have the opportunity to present evidence to the court that nondisclosure of identifying information is of greater benefit to the birth parent than disclosure to the adopted person.
- Any objection filed by the birth parent shall become invalid when withdrawn by the birth parent or when the birth parent dies.

Access to Adoption Records

Upon receipt of a death record for the birth parent, the agency shall release the identifying information to the adopted person if requested.

Access to Original Birth Certificate
Citation: Ann. Stat. § 259.89

An adopted person who is age 19 or older may request the Commissioner of Health to disclose the information on his or her original birth record. Within 5 days, the commissioner shall notify the Department of Human Services or child-placing agency of the request. Within 6 months after receiving the request, the department or agency shall make reasonable efforts to notify each birth parent.

If the department is unable to notify a parent identified on the original birth record within 6 months, and if neither parent has at any time filed an unrevoked consent to disclosure, the information may be disclosed as follows:

- If the person was adopted prior to August 1, 1977, he or she may petition the court for disclosure, and the court shall grant the petition if, after consideration of the interests of all known persons involved, the court determines that disclosure of the information would be of greater benefit than nondisclosure.
- If the person was adopted on or after August 1, 1977, the commissioner shall release the information to the adopted person.

If either birth parent has ever filed with the commissioner an unrevoked affidavit stating that the information on the original birth record should not be disclosed, the commissioner shall not disclose the information until the affidavit is revoked by the filing of a consent to disclosure by that parent.

If a parent named on the original birth record has died, and at any time prior to the death the parent has filed an unrevoked affidavit stating that the information not be disclosed, the adopted person may petition the court of original jurisdiction of the adoption proceeding for disclosure.

The State Registrar shall provide a copy of an adopted person's original birth record to an authorized representative of a federally recognized American Indian Tribe for the sole purpose of determining the adopted person's eligibility for enrollment or membership in the Tribe.

Where the Information Can Be Located

Adoption Archive, Minnesota Department of Health (Child Safety and Permanency Division, Adoption Assistance Program)

Mississippi

Who May Access Information
Citation: Ann. Code § 93-17-207
Nonidentifying information may be provided to:

- The adopted person who is age 18 or older
- The adoptive parent
- The legal guardian or custodian of an adopted person
- The offspring or birth sibling of an adopted person if the requester is age 18 or older

Identifying information is available to the adopted person who is age 21 or older.

Access to Nonidentifying Information
Citation: Ann. Code §§ 93-17-205; 93-17-207; 93-17-209
The Bureau of Vital Statistics shall maintain a centralized adoption records file for all adoptions performed in this State after July 1, 2005 that shall include the following information:

- The medical and social history of the birth parents, including information regarding genetically inheritable diseases and any similar information about the adopted person's grandparents, aunts, uncles, brothers, and sisters, if known
- A report of any medical examination that either birth parent had within 1 year before the date of the petition for adoption, if available and known
- A report describing the adopted person's prenatal care and medical condition at birth, if available and known
- The medical and social history of the adopted person, including information regarding genetically inheritable diseases, and any other relevant medical, social, and genetic information, if available

Any birth parent may file with the bureau at any time any relevant supplemental nonidentifying information about the adopted person or the birth parents, and the bureau shall maintain this information in the centralized adoption records file.

Access to Adoption Records

Nonidentifying information shall be released for a reasonable fee to any qualified person listed above. If the information is not on file, the adopted person may request the bureau to locate the birth parent and obtain the information.

If an agency receives a report from a physician that a birth parent or another child of the birth parent may have a genetically transferable disease, the agency shall notify the adopted person of the existence of the disease if he or she is age 21 or older, or the adopted person's guardian, custodian, or adoptive parent if he or she is under age 21. If an agency receives a report from a physician that an adopted person may have a genetically transferable disease, the agency shall notify the adopted person's birth parent of the existence of the disease.

Mutual Access to Identifying Information
Citation: Ann. Code §§ 93-17-205; 93-17-215; 93-17-217; 93-17-219

The bureau shall maintain as part of the centralized adoption records file the following:

- The name, date of birth, Social Security number (both original and revised, where applicable), and birth certificate (both original and revised) of the adopted person
- The names, current addresses, and Social Security numbers of the adopted person's birth parents, guardian, and legal custodian
- Any other available information about the birth parent's identity and location

The birth parent may file with the bureau at any time an affidavit authorizing the bureau to provide the adopted person with his or her original birth certificate and with any other available information about the birth parent's identity and location, or an affidavit expressly prohibiting the bureau from releasing any information about his or her identity and location, and prohibiting any licensed adoption agency from conducting a search for such birth parent. An affidavit filed under this section may be revoked at any time by written notification to the bureau.

An adopted person age 21 or older may request identifying information regarding either birth parent, unless that birth parent has executed an affidavit prohibiting the release of such information. The adopted person must submit to counseling in connection with any release.

If an affidavit is not on file, the adopted person may request the agency to undertake a search for the birth parent who has not filed an affidavit.

54 Child Welfare Information Gateway

Access to Original Birth Certificate
Citation: Ann. Code §§ 93-17-21; 93-17-205
The original birth certificate shall not be a public record and shall not be divulged except upon the order of the court or pursuant to §§ 93-17-201 through 93-17-223.

The birth parent may file with the bureau at any time an affidavit authorizing the bureau to provide the adopted person with his or her original birth certificate, or an affidavit expressly prohibiting the release of any information. The affidavit may be revoked at any time by written notification to the bureau.

Where the Information Can Be Located

- Mississippi Department of Health, Vital Records
- The licensed agency involved in the adoption

Missouri

Who May Access Information
Citation: Ann. Stat. § 453.121
Nonidentifying information is available to:

- The adoptive parents
- The child's legal guardians
- The adult adopted person
- The adult adopted person's lineal descendants if the adopted person is deceased

Identifying information is available to the adult adopted person or the adult adopted person's lineal descendants if the adopted person is deceased.

Access to Nonidentifying Information
Citation: Ann. Stat. § 453.121
Nonidentifying information, if known, concerning undisclosed birth parents or siblings shall be provided upon written request. Nonidentifying information can include the physical description, nationality, religious background, and medical history of the birth parents or siblings.

Mutual Access to Identifying Information
Citation: Ann. Stat. § 453.121

Access to Adoption Records

An adult adopted person, or his or her lineal descendants if he or she is deceased, may make a written request to the court for information identifying his or her birth parents. If the birth parents have consented to the release of identifying information, the court shall disclose that information. If the birth parents have not consented to the release of the information, the court shall, within 10 days of receipt of the request, notify in writing the child-placing agency or juvenile court having access to the requested information.

If the agency or court is unable to notify the birth parent within 3 months, the identifying information shall not be disclosed to the adult adopted person. If an affidavit executed by a birth parent authorizing the release of information is filed with the court, the court shall disclose the identifying information.

Any adult adopted person whose adoption was finalized in this State, or whose birth parents had their parental rights terminated in this State, may request the court to secure and disclose identifying information concerning an adult sibling. Identifying information pertaining exclusively to the adult sibling, whether part of the permanent record of a file in the court or in an agency, shall be released only upon consent of that adult sibling.

The department shall maintain a registry for birth parents, adult siblings, and adult adopted persons to indicate their desire to be contacted by each other. At the time of registration, a birth parent or adult sibling may consent in writing to the release of identifying information to an adult adopted person. If such consent has not been executed and the division believes that a match has occurred, the division shall make confidential contact with the birth parents or adult siblings and with the adult adopted person.

The birth parent, adult sibling, or adult adopted person may refuse to go forward with any further contact between the parties when contacted by the division.

Access to Original Birth Certificate
Citation: Ann. Stat. § 193.125

The State Registrar shall file the original certificate of birth with the certificate of decree of adoption and such file may be opened by the State Registrar only upon receipt of a certified copy of an order as decreed by the court of adoption.

Where the Information Can Be Located

Missouri Division of Family Services, Adoption Information Registry

Montana

Who May Access Information
Citation: Ann. Code § 42-6-102
The Department of Public Health and Human Services or an authorized person or agency may disclose:

- Nonidentifying information to an adopted person, an adoptive or birth parent, or an extended family member of an adopted or birth parent
- Identifying information to a court-appointed confidential intermediary upon order of the court or as provided in §§ 50-15-121 and 50-15-122
- Identifying information limited to the specific information required to assist an adopted person to become enrolled in or a member of an Indian Tribe
- Identifying information to authorized personnel during a Federal Child and Family Services Review
- An original birth certificate as provided for in § 42-6-109

Access to Nonidentifying Information
Citation: Ann. Code § 42-6-102
Upon request, all nonidentifying information will be provided to a person listed above.

Mutual Access to Identifying Information
Citation: Ann. Code §§ 42-6-102; 42-6-103; 42-6-104
Information may be disclosed to any person who consents in writing to the release of confidential information to other interested persons who have also consented. Identifying information pertaining to an adoption involving an adopted person who is still a child may not be disclosed based upon a consensual exchange of information unless the adopted person's adoptive parent consents in writing.

An adult adopted person, an adoptive or birth parent, or an adult extended family member may petition the court for disclosure of identifying information regarding the adopted person, a birth child, a birth parent, or an extended family member.

After a petition has been filed, the court shall appoint a confidential intermediary who shall conduct a confidential search for the person being sought. If the intermediary locates the person being sought, a confidential inquiry must be made as to whether the located person consents to having his or her present identity disclosed to the petitioner. If the person being sought does not consent, identifying information regarding that person may be disclosed only upon order of the court for good cause shown. If the person being sought is found to be deceased, the court may order disclosure of identifying information to the petitioner.

Access to Original Birth Certificate
Citation: Ann. Code § 42-6-109

In addition to any copy of an adopted person's original birth certificate authorized for release by a court order issued pursuant to § 50-15-121 or 50-15-122, the department shall furnish a copy of the original birth certificate of an adopted person:

- Upon the written request of a person who was adopted before October 1, 1985, or 30 years or more ago, whichever date is later
- Upon a court order for a person adopted on or after October 1, 1985, and before October 1, 1997
- For a person adopted on or after October 1, 1997, upon:
  - The written request of an adopted person who has reached age 18 unless the birth parent has requested in writing that the original birth certificate not be automatically released
  - A court order

A birth parent may request in writing to the Vital Statistics Bureau that the birth certificate for an adopted person not be released without a court order. The birth parent may change the request at any time by notifying the Vital Statistics Bureau in writing of the change.

The department may release a copy of the adopted person's original birth certificate if release of this document is required to assist an adopted person to become enrolled in or a member of an Indian Tribe.

Where the Information Can Be Located

Office of Vital Statistics, Montana Department of Public Health and Human Services

Nebraska

Who May Access Information
Citation: Rev. Stat. §§ 43-128; 43-130; 43-146.02; 43-146.04

Medical history shall be provided to:

- The adoptive parents
- The adopted person

Identifying information is available to:

- An adopted person who is age 25 or older for adoptions finalized prior to September 1, 1998
- An adopted person who is age 21 or older for adoptions finalized on or after September 1, 1998

Access to Nonidentifying Information
Citation: Rev. Stat. §§ 43-128; 43-146.02
A child-placing agency, the Department of Health and Human Services, or a private agency handling the adoption, as the case may be, shall maintain and shall provide to the adopting parents upon placement of the child and to the adopted person, upon his or her request, the available medical history of the adopted person and of the birth parents. The medical history shall not include the names of the birth parents, the child's place of birth, or any other identifying information.

Mutual Access to Identifying Information
Citation: Rev. Stat. §§ 43-131; 43-146.05
For adoptions finalized prior to September 1, 1998: Upon a request for information, the department shall check the records of the adopted person to determine whether a consent form has been signed and filed by any relative and whether an unrevoked nonconsent form is on file from a birth parent or an adoptive parent.

If the consent form has been signed and filed and not been revoked, and if no nonconsent form has been filed by an adoptive parent, the department shall release the information to the adopted person.

If no consent forms have been filed or if the consent form has been revoked, and if no nonconsent form has been filed, the following information shall be released to the adopted person:

Access to Adoption Records

- The name and address of the court that issued the adoption decree
- The name and address of any child-placing agency involved in the adoption
- The fact that an agency may assist the adopted person in searching for relatives

For adoptions finalized on or after September 1, 1998: Upon a request for information, the department shall check the records of the adopted person to determine whether an unrevoked nonconsent form is on file from a birth parent. If no nonconsent form has been filed, the following information shall be released to the adopted person:

- The name and address of the court that issued the adoption decree
- The name and address of any child-placing agency involved in the adoption
- The fact that an agency or the department may assist the adopted person in searching for relatives
- A copy of the adopted person's original birth certificate
- A copy of the adopted person's medical history and any medical records on file

If an unrevoked nonconsent form has been filed, no information may be released to the adopted person except a copy of his or her medical history, if requested. The medical history shall not include the names of the birth parents or relatives of the adopted person or any other identifying information.

Access to Original Birth Certificate
Citation: Rev. Stat. §§ 43-130; 43-136; 43-143; 43-146.04

For adoptions finalized prior to September 1, 1998, an adopted person who is age 25 or older may file a written request for the original birth certificate. For adoptions finalized on or after September 1, 1998, an adopted person who is age 21 or older may request the original birth certificate. If a consent form has been signed and filed by both birth parents, or by the birth mother of a child born out of wedlock, and no nonconsent form has been filed, a copy of the adopted person's original birth certificate shall be provided to the adopted person.

For adoptions finalized prior to July 20, 2002, an adoptive parent or parents may at any time file a notice of nonconsent stating that at no time prior to his or her death, or the death of both parents if each signed the form, may

60   Child Welfare Information Gateway

any information on the adopted person's original birth certificate be released to such adopted person.

Where the Information Can Be Located

Nebraska Department of Health and Human Services, Division of Children and Family Services—Adoption Searches

Nevada

Who May Access Information
Citation: Rev. Stat. §§ 127.007; 127.152
Information from the State register is available to:

- The adopted person who is age 18 or older
- The birth parents
- Persons related within the third degree to the adopted person

Medical and sociological information shall be provided to the adoptive parents.

Access to Nonidentifying Information
Citation: Rev. Stat. § 127.152
The agency that provides child welfare services or a licensed child-placing agency shall provide the adopting parents with a report that includes:

- A copy of any of the child's medical records that are in the possession of the agency
- Any information about the medical and sociological history of the child and the birth parents and any behavioral, emotional, or psychological problems that the child may have
- Information regarding any subsidies, assistance, and other services that may be available to the child if it is determined that he or she has any special needs

The report must exclude any information that would lead to the identification of the birth parent.

Mutual Access to Identifying Information
Citation: Rev. Stat. § 127.007
The division shall maintain the State register for adoptions to provide information to identify adults who were adopted and persons related to them

Access to Adoption Records 61

within the third degree of consanguinity. The State register for adoptions consists of:

- Names and other information relating to persons who have released a child for adoption and who have submitted the information voluntarily to the division
- Names and other necessary information of persons who are 18 years of age or older who were adopted and who have submitted the information voluntarily to the division
- Names and other necessary information of persons who are related within the third degree of consanguinity to adopted persons and who have submitted the information voluntarily to the division

Any person whose name appears in the register may withdraw it by requesting in writing that it be withdrawn. The division shall immediately withdraw a name upon receiving the request and may not thereafter release any information to identify that person, including the information that such a name was ever in the register.

The division may release information about a person related within the third degree of consanguinity to an adopted person, or about an adopted person to a person related within the third degree of consanguinity, if the names and information about both persons are contained in the register and if written consent for the release of such information is given by the birth parent.

Access to Original Birth Certificate
Citation: Rev. Stat. § 440.310
The original birth certificate is available only upon order of the court.

Where the Information Can Be Located
Nevada Adoption Registry Services, Division of Child and Family Services

New Hampshire

Who May Access Information
Citation: Rev. Stat. §§ 170:B-23; 170:B-24
Nonidentifying information is available to:

- The adopted person who is age 18 or older
- The birth parents

- The adoptive parents

Identifying information is available to:

- The adopted person
- The birth parents
- Blood relatives

Access to Nonidentifying Information
Citation: Rev. Stat. §§ 170:B-23; 170:B-24
The department or the licensed child-placing agency may share with the adoptive parents all information it has available about the minor child being placed for adoption. The department or the licensed child-placing agency shall delete any information that would tend to identify a birth parent.

Requests for nonidentifying social or medical information may be made by an adopted person who is age 18 or older, a parent of an adopted person under the age of 18, or a birth parent.

When any person listed above submits a request for nonidentifying social or medical information, the department or agency shall disclose such information relating to the adopted person, the birth parents, or the blood relatives. The department or the agency shall delete any information from the health history or background that would tend to be identifying. Court approval is not required for information disclosed under this paragraph.

Mutual Access to Identifying Information
Citation: Rev. Stat. § 170:B-24
If the parties mutually agree to the release of identifying information, it shall be released as provided in this paragraph. Only the following people may authorize the disclosure of identifying information about an adopted person, a birth parent, or a blood relative:

- An adopted person who is age 18 or older
- The adoptive parents of an adopted person under age 18
- A birth parent, who can authorize the disclosure of identifying information at the time of surrender or later

Any release may be revoked or amended at any time. The person signing the release or its revocation shall file a copy with the department or licensed child-placing agency. The department or licensed child-placing agency shall then file a copy of the release with the court that heard the adoption petition.

Court approval is not required for release of identifying information when a release has been signed, and the person affirms his or her desire to be contacted.

Court approval shall be required if the parties do not agree, if they cannot be contacted, or if the department or agency questions the safety of releasing information.

Access to Original Birth Certificate
Citation: Rev. Stat. § 170:B-23
The original birth certificate is subject to inspection only upon written order of the court for good cause shown.

Where the Information Can Be Located
New Hampshire Department of State, Division of Vital Records

New Jersey

Who May Access Information
Citation: Ann. Stat. §§ 9:3-41.1; 26:8-40.34
The adoptive parent may have access to nonidentifying information.

The birth parent may authorize the release of identifying information to the adopted person.

Access to Nonidentifying Information
Citation: Ann. Stat. §§ 9:3-41.1; 9:3-39.2; 9:3-39.3
Prior to placement, the adoptive parent will be provided with all available information relevant to the child's development, including:

- The child's developmental and medical history
- The child's personality and temperament
- The birth parents' complete medical histories, including conditions or diseases that are believed to be hereditary
- Any drugs or medications taken during pregnancy
- Any other health conditions of the birth parents that may influence the child's present or future health

Information that would identify or permit the identification of the birth parents of the child shall be excluded.

In the event that the adopted person was under the care and custody of the Division of Child Protection and Permanency in the Department of Children

64 Child Welfare Information Gateway

and Families at the time of the person's adoption, the director of the division shall provide, upon request by an authorized requester, a statement providing summaries of the medical and social characteristics of birth family members, family health histories, the facts and circumstances related to adoptive placement, and summaries of case record material.

An authorized requester may request that the adoption facilitator who placed the child for adoption or conducted an investigation provide any available nonidentifying family medical history information concerning the adopted person contained in that person's confidential case records maintained by the adoption facilitator. Upon receipt of a request, the adoption facilitator shall provide the requester with a detailed summary of any available nonidentifying family medical history information concerning the adopted person that is contained in that person's confidential case records.

Mutual Access to Identifying Information
Citation: Ann. Stat. § 26:8-40.34

A birth parent of an adopted person may submit a contact preference form to the State Registrar indicating the birth parent's preference regarding contact with the adopted person. The birth parent may change his or her preference at any time by submitting a revised document to the registrar. The registrar shall require a birth parent who submits a contact preference form to simultaneously submit a completed form providing updated family history information, including medical, cultural, and social history information.

On the contact preference form, the birth parent may select one of the following options:

- Direct contact
- Contact through an intermediary
- No contact

The registrar shall request a birth parent who indicates a preference for no contact by the adopted person to update the family history information every 10 years until the birth parent reaches age 40, and every 5 years thereafter.

The registrar shall maintain a file of documents of contact preference and family history information submitted by birth parents. Upon request for an original certificate of birth, the registrar shall determine whether there are contact preference forms and family history information documents regarding the adopted person on file, and if those documents exist, shall place and retain them in the adopted person's original certificate of birth file. Those documents

Access to Adoption Records   65

shall be released when a request is made for an uncertified, long- form copy of an adopted person's original certificate of birth.

In the case of a person adopted prior to August 1, 2015, a birth parent may submit a request on or before December 31, 2016 that provides that the name and other identifying information of the birth parent shall be redacted in response to a request for information. The birth parent may rescind the redaction request at any time.

Access to Original Birth Certificate
Citation: Ann. Stat. §§ 26:8-40.1; 26:8-40.33

Effective until January 1, 2017: The State Registrar shall place under seal the original certificate of birth and all papers pertaining to the new certificate of birth. The seal shall not be broken except by order of a court of competent jurisdiction.

Effective January 1, 2017: Upon receipt of a request pursuant to § 26:8-40.1(c), the State Registrar shall provide the authorized requester with an uncertified, long-form copy of the adopted person's original certificate of birth.

Where the Information Can Be Located
New Jersey Department of Children and Families, Adoption Registry

New Mexico

Who May Access Information
Citation: Ann. Stat. § 32A-5-40
Information may be accessed by:

- The adopted person who is age 18 or older
- The birth parent if the adopted person is age 18 or older
- The adoptive parent of an adopted person under age 18
- An adopted person's birth sibling
- A guardian
- An attorney for any party

Access to Nonidentifying Information
Citation: Ann. Stat. § 32A-5-40
Unless the birth parent and the adopted person have consented to the release of their identities, inspection of records is limited to nonidentifying information. This includes:

66 Child Welfare Information Gateway

- The health and medical histories of the birth parents and the adopted person
- General family background
- Physical descriptions
- The length of time the adopted person was in the care and custody of persons other than the adoptive parents

Mutual Access to Identifying Information
Citation: Ann. Stat. §§ 32A-5-40; 32A-5-41
At any time after the entry of the decree of adoption, a birth parent may file:

- Consent or refusal to be contacted
- Release of the birth parent's identity to the adult adopted person or to the adoptive parent of a minor adopted person
- Information regarding the birth parent's location or changes in background information

At any time, an adult adopted person may file information regarding his or her location and consent or refusal regarding opening of his or her adoption file to his or her birth parents.

If mutual authorizations for release of identifying information by the parties are not available, an adult adopted person, the birth parents, or the adoptive parents if the adopted person is a minor may file a motion with the court to obtain the release of identifying information for good cause shown. When hearing the motion, the court shall give primary consideration to the best interests of the adopted person, but shall also give due consideration to the interests of the members of the adopted person's birth and adoptive families. The court may assign a confidential intermediary to ascertain needed information.

An adopted person shall have the right to access information to enroll in his or her Tribe of origin. If the department establishes that an adopted person is of Indian descent, the department shall:

- Provide the requester with the Tribal affiliation of the adopted person's birth parents
- Submit to the Tribe information necessary to establish Tribal enrollment for the adopted person and to protect any rights flowing from the adopted person's Tribal relationship

Access to Adoption Records

- Provide notice to the requester of the department's submission of information to the adopted person's Tribe

Access to Original Birth Certificate
Citation: Ann. Stat. § 24-14-17
The original birth certificate is available only upon order of the court.
Where the Information Can Be Located
New Mexico Adoption Search, Department of Children, Youth and Families

New York

Who May Access Information
Citation: Pub. Health Law §§ 4138-c; 4138-d
The following persons may receive information:

- The adopted person who is age 18 or older
- The birth parents
- A birth sibling who is age 18 or older

Access to Nonidentifying Information
Citation: Pub. Health Law §§ 4138-c; 4138-d
The Department of Health shall operate an adoption information registry for the exchange of nonidentifying information between the persons listed above. Nonidentifying information shall include only the following information, if known, about the adopted person, birth parents, and birth siblings:

- The age of the parents in years at the time of the child's birth
- The heritage of the parents, including nationality, ethnic background, race, and religion
- Education completed by the parents at the time of the child's birth
- General physical appearance of the parents at the time of the child's birth, including height, weight, color of hair, eyes, skin, and other information of similar nature
- The occupation of the parents
- The health history of the parents
- The talents, hobbies, and special interests of the parents

68 Child Welfare Information Gateway

- The facts and circumstances relating to the adoption
- The existence of any known birth siblings
- The number, sex, and age, at the time of the adopted person's adoption, of any known birth siblings

Upon acceptance of a registration, the department shall search registry records to determine whether the adopted person's adoption occurred within the State. If the adoption did occur within the State, the department shall request nonidentifying information from court records. If the department determines that the adoption did not occur within the State, it shall notify the registrant that no record exists of the adoption occurring within the State.

If an agency was involved in the adoption, nonidentifying information may be accessed by registering the mutual consent voluntary adoption registry maintained by the agency.

Mutual Access to Identifying Information
Citation: Pub. Health Law §§ 4138-c; 4138-d
The department shall operate an adoption information registry for the exchange of information among the persons listed above. Any person whose registration was accepted may withdraw the registration prior to the release of any identifying information.

Upon acceptance of a registration, the department shall search the registry files to determine whether the person sought is registered. If there is a match, the department shall notify the court to request the person's final consent to the release of identifying information.

Upon receipt of a final consent by the adopted person, birth parent, and/or birth sibling, the department shall, unless the adopted person or birth sibling has elected otherwise, release identifying information to all the registrants. Such identifying information shall be limited to the names and addresses of the registrants and shall not include any other information contained in the adoption or birth records.

A mutual consent voluntary adoption registry may be maintained by each agency involved in an adoption. Persons eligible to receive identifying information may work through the agency involved in the adoption. The agency shall accept and maintain the registrations of an adopted person, the birth parents, or a birth sibling. If the agency determines that the agency was involved in the adoption, it shall transmit the registration to the adoption information registry operated by the department and release nonidentifying information.

Access to Adoption Records 69

An adoption medical information subregistry shall be part of the registry. Access to all identifying records and information in the subregistry shall be subject to the same restrictions as the adoption information registry. The department shall establish procedures by which a birth parent may provide medical information to the subregistry, and by which an adopted person age 18 or older, or the adoptive parents of an adopted person who is under age 18, may access the medical information.

Access to Original Birth Certificate
Citation: Pub. Health Law § 4138
The original birth certificate is available only upon order of the court.

Where the Information Can Be Located
New York State Department of Health, Adoption Registry

North Carolina

Who May Access Information
Citation: Gen. Stat. §§ 48-9-103; 48-9-104; 48-9-109
Nonidentifying information is available to:

- The adoptive parent
- The adult adopted person
- A minor adopted person who is a parent or an expectant parent

A licensed child-placing agency or a county Department of Social Services may agree to act as a confidential intermediary for the purpose of sharing identifying information for any of the following:

- A birth parent
- An adult adopted person
- An adult birth sibling of an adult adopted person
- An adult birth half-sibling of an adult adopted person
- An adult family member of a deceased birth parent
- An adult family member of a deceased adopted person

Access to Nonidentifying Information
Citation: Gen. Stat. §§ 48-9-103; 48-3-205
Any person listed above may request a copy of any document prepared pursuant to § 48-3-205 and any additional nonidentifying health-related

70 Child Welfare Information Gateway

information about the adopted person's original family. The information that is provided at the time of the adoptive placement includes:

- The date of the child's birth and any other reasonably available nonidentifying information
- The age of the birth parents at the time of the child's birth
- The heritage of the birth parents, including nationality, ethnic background, and race
- Education completed by the birth parents at the time of the child's birth
- The general physical appearance of the birth parents
- All reasonably available nonidentifying information about the health and genetic history of the child, the birth parents, and other members of the birth parents' families

Nonidentifying information about the adopted person's present circumstances may be disclosed to a birth parent, an adult sibling, or the guardian of a minor sibling.

Mutual Access to Identifying Information
Citation: Gen. Stat. §§ 48-9-104; 48-9-109

Except as provided below, no one shall release from any sealed records the name, address, or other identifying information about an adopted person, adoptive parent, birth parent, or individual who, but for the adoption, would be the adopted person's sibling or grandparent, except upon order of the court.

A child-placing agency may agree to act as a confidential intermediary for a person listed above without appointment by the court in order to obtain and share nonidentifying birth family health information, facilitate contact, or share identifying information with the written consent of all parties. An agency also may agree to act as a confidential intermediary for the adoptive parents of a minor adopted person without appointment to obtain and share nonidentifying birth family health information.

If such agency determines that the person who is the subject of the search, or a lineal ascendant of that person, is deceased, the agency may obtain a copy of the death certificate and deliver it to the person who requested the services.

Nothing in this article is meant to prevent:

- An employee of a court, agency, or any other person from:
  - Inspecting confidential records, other than records maintained by the State Registrar, for the purpose of discharging any obligation

Access to Adoption Records 71

- Disclosing the name of the court or agency involved in the adoption to an individual described above who can verify his or her identity
- Disclosing or using information contained in sealed records for statistical or research purposes
- In agency placements, a parent placing a child for adoption and the adopting parents from authorizing an agency to release information to each other that may reveal the identity of an adopted person, an adoptive parent, or an adopted person's placing parent
- The Division of Social Services from sharing information regarding the identity of birth parents with an agency acting as a confidential intermediary

Access to Original Birth Certificate
Citation: Gen. Stat. § 48-9-106
Upon receipt of a certified copy of a court order issued pursuant to § 48-9-105 authorizing the release of an adopted person's original birth certificate, the State Registrar shall give the individual who obtained the order a copy of the original birth certificate with a certification that the copy is a true copy of a record that is no longer a valid certificate of birth.
Where the Information Can Be Located
North Carolina Department of Health and Human Services, Division of Social Services

North Dakota

Who May Access Information
Citation: Cent. Code § 14-15-16
Nonidentifying information must be provided to:

- The adoptive parents
- The adult adopted person
- The birth parent

Identifying information may be provided to:

- The birth parents
- The adoptive parents

Child Welfare Information Gateway

- The adopted person
- Adult birth siblings
- The adult child of an adopted person

Access to Nonidentifying Information
Citation: Cent. Code § 14-15-16; 14-15-01(12)
Nonidentifying information, if known, concerning undisclosed birth parents must be furnished upon written request to the individuals listed above. The term 'nonidentifying adoptive information' includes:

- The age of the birth parent at the time of the child's birth
- The heritage and religion of the birth parent
- The education completed by the birth parent at the time of the child's birth
- The general physical appearance of birth parent at the time of the child's birth, including the height, weight, color of hair, eyes, skin, and other information of a similar nature
- The talents, hobbies, and special interests of the birth parents
- The existence of any other children born to either birth parent
- The reasons for the child being placed for adoption
- The vocation of the birth parent in general terms
- The health history of the birth parents and blood relatives

Mutual Access to Identifying Information
Citation: Cent. Code § 14-15-16
Before the child reaches adulthood, exchanges of identifying information may take place between the birth parents, adoptive parents, and adopted person. Disclosure of a party's identifying information may not occur unless the party consents to disclosure. If one parent objects, the identifying information disclosed by the agency may only relate to the consenting parent or parents.

An adopted person who is age 18 or older may request the department to initiate the disclosure of information identifying his or her birth parents or adult birth sibling. A birth parent or adult birth sibling may request the department to initiate the disclosure of information identifying that individual. An adult child of an adopted person may request the department to initiate the disclosure of information identifying the adopted person's birth parents.

Within 90 days after receiving a request, the child-placing agency shall make complete and reasonable efforts to notify the individual or individuals that a disclosure of identifying information has been requested. An adopted person, birth parent, or birth sibling may authorize disclosure, refuse to authorize disclosure, or take no action. If no action is taken in response to a request, the child-placing agency must treat that as a refusal to authorize disclosure, except that it does not preclude disclosure after the person's death.

Upon application to the department by an adult adopted person or the parent or guardian of a minor adopted person, the department may investigate to determine the adopted person's eligibility for enrollment as a member of an Indian Tribe.

Access to Original Birth Certificate
Citation: Cent. Code § 23-02.1-18
The original birth record is available only upon order of a court or as provided by rules and regulations.

Where the Information Can Be Located
North Dakota Department of Human Services, Adoption Search/ Disclosure

Northern Mariana Islands

Who May Access Information
Citation: Comm. Code Tit. 8, § 1414
The adoptive parent or the adopted child may consent to release of information.

Access to Nonidentifying Information
The issue is not addressed in the statutes reviewed.

Mutual Access to Identifying Information
Citation: Comm. Code Tit. 8, § 1414
All papers and records pertaining to the adoption are subject to inspection only upon consent of the court and all interested persons. The identity of an adoptive parent or child may not be disclosed except by consent in writing of the adoptive parent, the adopted child who is age 14 years or older, or upon order of the court for good cause in exceptional cases.

Access to Original Birth Certificate
Citation: Comm. Code Tit. 8, §§ 1414; 1417
The original birth certificate is sealed as part of the adoption record and may be opened only as provided by Tit.8, § 1414.

Where the Information Can Be Located
The agency involved in the adoption

Ohio

Who May Access Information
Citation: Rev. Code §§ 3107.66; 3107.47; 3107.49
Nonidentifying information is available to:

- An adopted person who is age 18 or older
- An adoptive parent of an adopted person who is under age 18
- An adoptive family member of a deceased adopted person
- A birth parent of an adopted person who is age 18 or older
- A birth sibling who is age 18 or older
- A birth family member if the birth parent is deceased

Identifying information is accessible to:

- An adopted person who is age 21 or older
- An adoptive parent of an adopted person who is older than age 18 but younger than 21
- The birth parent or adult birth sibling

Access to Nonidentifying Information
Citation: Rev. Code §§ 3107.66; 3107.60
An adopted person, an adoptive parent, or an adoptive family member may submit a written request to the agency or attorney who arranged the adoption or the probate court that finalized the adoption, for nonidentifying information about the adoptee person's birth parent or birth sibling contained in the agency's, attorney's, or court's adoption records.

A birth parent, birth sibling, or birth family member may submit a written request for nonidentifying information about the adopted person or adoptive parent.

The term 'nonidentifying information' means one of the following:

- In relation to a birth parent, any information that is not identifying information, including all of the following:
  - A birth parent's age at the time the child was adopted
  - The medical and genetic history of the birth parents
  - The age, sex, and medical and genetic history of an adopted person's birth siblings and extended family members

Access to Adoption Records

- A person's heritage and ethnic background, educational level, general physical appearance, religion, occupation, and cause of death
- Any information that may be included in a social and medical history as specified § 3107.09(B)-(C)
- In relation to an adoptive parent, any information that is not identifying information, including all of the following:
  - An adoptive parent's age at the time of adoption
  - An adoptive sibling's age at the time of adoption
  - The heritage, ethnic background, religion, educational level, and occupation of the adoptive parent
  - General information known about the well-being of the adopted person before and after the adoption

Mutual Access to Identifying Information
Citation: Rev. Code §§ 3107.47; 3107.49

For adoptions completed before January 1, 1964, adopted persons have access upon request to the adoption file maintained by the Department of Health.

For adoptions completed between 1964 and 1996:

- Any birth parent or sibling who wishes to authorize the release of identifying information shall file a release form with the department. A release may be filed with the department at any time. The department shall establish and maintain a file of releases.
- At age 21, an adopted person may file a petition with the Probate Court that finalized his or her adoption and inquire if a release form has been filed. In the event of a match, identifying information may be released to the adopted person.
- The court that decreed the adoption may order that the contents of the adoption file be made open for inspection or available for copying.

For adoptions completed after 1996:

- A birth parent may file with the department a denial of release form that shall be placed in the adoption file. The birth parent may rescind an authorization of release form and rescind a denial of release form as many times as the birth parent wishes.

- An adopted person age 21 or older, or an adoptive parent of an adopted person at least age 18 but under age 21, may submit a request to the Department of Health for a copy of the contents of the adopted person's adoption file. If there is not an effective denial of release form for either birth parent in the adopted person's adoption file, the department shall provide the adopted person or adoptive parent a copy of the contents of the adopted person's adoption file.

Access to Original Birth Certificate
Citation: Rev. Code §§ 3705.12; 3705.126

Upon the issuance of the new birth record, the original birth record shall cease to be a public record. The department shall place the original birth record and the items sent by the probate court pursuant to § 3107.19 in an adoption file and seal the file. The contents of the adoption file are not a public record and shall be available only in accordance with § 3705.126. The contents of the adoption file include any contact preference form, birth parent's name redaction request form, or social and medical history accepted and maintained by the department.

The department shall neither open an adoption file nor make its contents available except as follows:

- The department shall inspect the file to determine the court involved.
- The department shall make the file's contents available to an adopted person or lineal descendant of an adopted person in accordance with § 3107.38.
- The department shall open the file to transfer releases to the file in accordance with § 3107.381.
- The department shall open the file to file a contact preference form from a birth parent and remove any previously filed contact preference form from the birth parent.
- The department shall open the file to file a birth parent's name redaction request form or to remove and destroy the form.
- The department shall open the file to file a denial of release form or an authorization of release form.
- The department shall make the file's contents available to an adopted person or adoptive parent in accordance with § 3107.47.
- The department shall open the file to file a request from an adopted person under § 3107.48 or to remove and destroy the request.

Access to Adoption Records 77

- The department shall inspect the file to assist a birth parent or birth sibling in finding the adopted person's name by adoption in accordance with § 3107.49.
- The court that decreed the adoption may order that the contents be made open for inspection or available for copying.

Where the Information Can Be Located
Ohio Department of Health, Adoption Information

Oklahoma

Who May Access Information
Citation: Ann. Stat. Tit. 10, § 7508-1.3
The services of a confidential intermediary are available to:

- The adult adopted person
- The legal parent or guardian of the child of a deceased adopted person
- The adult descendant of a deceased adopted person
- The birth parent
- The adult birth sibling or grandparent of an adult adopted person
- The sibling of a deceased birth parent

Access to Nonidentifying Information
Citation: Ann. Stat. Tit. 10, § 7508-1.3
If the person who is the subject of the search is not willing to share identifying information, meet, or communicate with the person who initiated the search, the confidential intermediary shall attempt to obtain any nonidentifying medical or social history information that has been requested by the person who has initiated the search.

If nonidentifying medical or social history information was obtained, the administrator shall provide a copy of the nonidentifying information to the person who initiated the search.

Mutual Access to Identifying Information
Citation: Ann. Stat. Tit. 10, §§ 7508-1.2; 7508-1.3
The department shall establish a search program using the services of a confidential intermediary that may be used by eligible persons listed above to locate an adult birth relative with whom contact has been lost through adoption.

If a birth relative of an adopted person, other than a birth parent, applies to initiate a search or is the subject of a search, the administrator of the confidential intermediary search program shall ascertain from the State Registrar of Vital Statistics whether an affidavit of nondisclosure by a birth parent is on file. If such an affidavit is on file and has not been revoked, the search may not be initiated.

The intermediary will conduct a reasonable search for an individual being sought and make a discreet and confidential inquiry as to whether the individual consents to the release of identifying information or medical information or to meeting or communicating with the individual initiating the search. If the individual initiating the search and the individual being sought consent in writing to meet or to communicate with each other, the intermediary will act to facilitate any meeting or communication between them.

If the confidential intermediary is able to locate the subject of the search, he or she shall make a discreet and confidential inquiry as to whether the person who is the subject of the search will consent to share identifying information, communicate, or meet with the person who initiated the search. The inquiry shall be by personal and confidential contact, without disclosing the identifying information about the person who initiated the search.

If the person who is the subject of the search is willing to share identifying information, communicate, or meet with the person who initiated the search, the confidential intermediary shall obtain this consent in writing.

Access to Original Birth Certificate
Citation: Ann. Stat. Tit. 10, § 7505-6.6
For adoptions finalized after November 1, 1997, an uncertified copy of the original birth certificate is available to an adopted person, age 18 or older, upon written request under the following conditions:

- He or she presents proof of identity.
- There are no birth siblings under age 18 who are currently in an adoptive family and whose whereabouts are known.
- The birth parents have not filed affidavits of nondisclosure.

Original birth certificates are also available upon order of the court for good cause shown, pursuant to § 7505-1.1.

Access to Adoption Records

Where the Information Can Be Located

- Adoption Reunion Registry, Oklahoma Department of Human Services
- Confidential Intermediary Search Program, Oklahoma Department of Human Services

Oregon

Who May Access Information
Citation: Ann. Stat. §§ 109.455; 109.500

The voluntary adoption registry may be used to obtain identifying information by the following persons:

- A birth parent
- An adult adopted person
- An adult birth sibling
- The adoptive parent of a deceased adopted person
- The parents or adult siblings of a deceased birth parent

Nonidentifying information may be released to:

- The adoptive parents of the child or the child's guardian
- The birth parent of the adopted person
- An adult adopted person
- If the adopted person is deceased:
  - The adopted person's spouse if the spouse is the birth parent of the adopted person's child or the guardian of any child of the adopted person
  - Any progeny of the adopted person who is age 18 or older

Access to Nonidentifying Information
Citation: Ann. Stat. § 109.500

A genetic, social, and health history that excludes information identifying any birth parent or putative father, member of a birth parent's or putative father's family, the adopted person or the adoptive parents of the adopted person may be provided, if available, from an agency upon request to the persons listed above.

80   Child Welfare Information Gateway

Mutual Access to Identifying Information
Citation: Ann. Stat. §§ 109.455; 109.460
The persons listed above may use the voluntary adoption registry for obtaining identifying information about birth parents, the putative father, the adult adopted person, and adult birth siblings. An adult adopted person who has a birth sibling in the adult adopted person's adoptive family who is under age 18 may not have access to the registry. A putative father may not have access to the registry.

The persons listed above shall work through the agency involved in the adoption, or its successor agency, or the Department of Human Services to receive information concerning the adoption.

The persons listed above and a putative father may register by submitting a signed affidavit to the registry. The affidavit shall contain the information listed in § 109.465 and a statement of the registrant's willingness to be identified to the other relevant persons who register. The affidavit gives authority to the registry to release identifying information to the other relevant persons who register. Each registration shall be accompanied by the registrant's certified copy of the record of live birth.

An adopted person, or the parent or guardian of an adopted person under age 18, may register to have specific identifying information disclosed to Indian Tribes or to governmental agencies in order to establish the adopted person's eligibility for Tribal membership or for benefits or to a person settling an estate.

If a birth parent or an adopted person fails to file an affidavit with the registry for any reason, including death or disability, identifying information shall not be disclosed.

Access to Original Birth Certificate
Citation: Ann. Stat. § 432.228
Upon receipt of a written application to the State Registrar, any adopted person age 21 and older born in the State of Oregon shall be issued a certified copy of his or her unaltered, original, and unamended certificate of birth that is in the custody of the State Registrar, with procedures, filing fees, and waiting periods identical to those imposed upon nonadopted citizens.

A birth parent may at any time request from the State Registrar of the Center for Health Statistics or from a voluntary adoption registry a contact preference form that shall accompany a birth certificate issued under the section above. The contact preference form shall provide the following information, to be completed at the option of the birth parent:

Access to Adoption Records

- I would like to be contacted.
- I would prefer to be contacted only through an intermediary.
- I prefer not to be contacted at this time. If I decide later that I would like to be contacted, I will register with the voluntary adoption registry. I have completed an updated medical history and have filed it with the voluntary adoption registry.

The certificate from the voluntary adoption registry verifying receipt of an updated medical history shall be in a form prescribed by the Oregon Health Authority and shall be supplied upon request of the birth parent by the voluntary adoption registry.

When the State Registrar receives a completed contact preference form from a birth parent, the State Registrar shall match the contact preference form with the adopted person's sealed file. The contact preference form shall be placed in the adopted person's sealed file when a match is made. A completed contact preference form shall be confidential.

Where the Information Can Be Located

Oregon Department of Human Services, Adoption Search and Registry Program

Pennsylvania

Who May Access Information
Citation: Cons. Stat. Tit. 23, §§ 2924; 2931

The following persons may request information from the registry, the court that finalized the adoption, or the agency that coordinated the adoption:

- An adopted person who is at least age 18
- An adoptive parent of an adopted person who is younger than 18, incapacitated, or deceased
- A legal guardian of an adopted person who is younger than 18 or incapacitated
- A descendant of a deceased adopted person
- The birth parent of an adopted person who is at least 21
- A parent of a birth parent of an adopted person who is at least 21 if the birth parent consents or is incapacitated or deceased
- A birth sibling of an adopted person, if both the birth sibling and adopted person are at least 21, and:

- The birth sibling remained in the custody of the birth parent and the birth parent consents or is deceased or incapacitated.
- Both the birth sibling and adopted person were adopted out of the same birth family.
- The birth sibling was not adopted out of the birth family and did not remain in the custody of the birth parent.

A person listed above may request nonidentifying or identifying information about or contact with the following persons:

- An adopted person who is age 21 or older
- A birth parent of an adopted person
- A parent of a birth parent of an adopted person who is age 21 or older, if the birth parent consents or is incapacitated or deceased
- A birth sibling of an adopted person, if both the birth sibling and the adopted person are age 21 or older, and:
  - The birth sibling remained in the custody of the birth parent and the birth parent consents or is deceased or incapacitated.
  - Both the birth sibling and adopted person were adopted out of the same birth family.
  - The birth sibling was not adopted out of the birth family and did not remain in the custody of the birth parent.

Access to Nonidentifying Information
Citation: Cons. Stat. Tit. 23, §§ 2925; 2932; 2934
Nonidentifying information available to the registry shall be provided to the requester within 30 days of the request. Before the release of information, the department shall remove any identifying information unless release has been authorized in writing by the subject of the information.

When the court or agency receives a written request for nonidentifying information, it shall, within 30 days, notify the requester of its receipt of the request. The court or agency shall, within 120 days, review its records and furnish to the requester any information concerning the adoption that will not compromise the confidentiality of the relationship between the adopted person and the adopted person's birth parent.

Medical and social history information may be filed with the court that terminated parental rights or finalized the adoption, the agency that coordinated the adoption, or the information registry.

Access to Adoption Records

The following persons may at any time file, update, and request medical and social history information:

- An adopted person who is age 18 or older
- An adoptive parent of an adopted person who is younger than 18 or incapacitated
- A descendant of a deceased adopted person
- A birth parent
- A legal guardian of an incapacitated birth parent
- A survivor of a deceased birth parent

When the court or agency receives a written request for medical and social history information, it shall notify the requester within 120 days whether it possesses any medical and social history information related to the adoption.

For nonidentifying information, the court or agency shall, within 120 days of locating the information, review and furnish to the requester any medical and social history information that will not compromise confidentiality.

If the requester is an adopted person seeking information about a birth parent who is deceased, any information on file regarding the deceased birth parent may be disclosed.

Mutual Access to Identifying Information
Citation: Cons. Stat. Tit. 23, §§ 2912; 2925; 2933; 2934

The Department of Public Welfare shall establish a statewide confidential registry for the retention of medical and social history information for all adoptions finalized or registered in the State.

For identifying information from the registry, if an authorization form is on file, the department shall notify the requester within 30 days whether information may be released. If there is no authorization on file, the department shall designate an authorized representative to use reasonable efforts to locate the subject of the request and obtain written authorization before any information is released.

An authorization form allowing the release of identifying information may be withdrawn at any time by the person who signed the form.

The court or agency, within 120 days of receiving a written request for identifying information or contact, shall determine whether it has any records relating to the adopted person and conduct a good faith search for identifying information. A representative shall review the court and agency record for identifying information regarding the birth or adoptive family and shall determine whether an authorization form has been filed.

If the requester is an adopted person seeking the identity of a birth parent, the identity of and any information about a deceased birth parent may be disclosed. If the requester is an adopted person seeking the identity of both birth parents and only one birth parent agrees to the disclosure, only the information relating to that birth parent shall be disclosed.

When the court or agency receives a written request for medical and social history information, it shall notify the requester within 120 days whether it possesses any information. For identifying information, if an authorization form is on file, the information will be released.

Access to Original Birth Certificate
Citation: Cons. Stat. Tit. 23, § 2937

No disclosure shall be made regarding an adopted person's original birth record or regarding the documents or proof on which an amended certificate of birth is based or relating in any way to the birth parents unless the disclosure is made pursuant to the provisions of this section.

The birth parents may, at the time their parental rights are terminated or at any time thereafter, place on file with the court and the Department of Health a consent form granting permission for the court or the department to issue a copy of the summary of the adopted person's original birth record, disclosing the identity of the birth parents, at any time after the adopted person turns age 18 or, if the adopted person is younger than age 18, to the adoptive parent or legal guardian.

If only one birth parent has filed a consent, a copy of the summary of the original birth record naming only the consenting birth parent shall be issued.

The consent of a birth parent may be withdrawn at any time by filing a withdrawal of consent form with the court and the Department of Health.

Where the Information Can Be Located
Pennsylvania Department of Health, Adoption Information Registry

Puerto Rico

Who May Access Information
This issue is not addressed in the statutes reviewed.
Access to Nonidentifying Information
This issue is not addressed in the statutes reviewed.
Mutual Access to Identifying Information
Citation: Ann. Laws Tit. 32; § 2699s

The adoption files shall be confidential. The court may only authorize the interested parties to examine them. It may also authorize other persons through a specific judicial order and for just cause.

Access to Original Birth Certificate
Citation: Ann. Laws Tit. 24, § 1136
The original birth certificate is available only upon order of the court.

Where the Information Can Be Located
Vital Statistics Registry

Rhode Island

Who May Access Information
Citation: Gen. Laws §§ 15-7.2-2; 15-7.2-7
The following persons may use the passive voluntary adoption reunion registry:

- Birth parents and adult birth siblings
- The adult adopted person
- Surviving relatives of a deceased adopted person
- The parent or adult sibling of a deceased birth parent
- The adoptive parent of a deceased adopted person

Access to Nonidentifying Information
Citation: Gen. Laws §§ 15-7.2-1; 15-7.2-2
The passive voluntary adoption reunion registry shall provide for the transmission of nonidentifying health, social, and genetic history of the adult adopted persons, birth parents, and other specified persons. Genetic and social history includes the following information that is available:

- Medical history
- Health status
- Cause of and age at death
- Height, weight, and eye and hair color
- Ethnic origins
- Religion, if any

Health history includes, when obtainable, the child's health status and medical history at the time of placement for adoption, including neonatal, psychological, developmental, physiological, and medical care history.

Mutual Access to Identifying Information
Citation: Gen. Laws §§ 15-7.2-2; 15-7.2-7; 15-7.2-9; 15-7.2-12; 5-7.2-14

The persons listed above may use the registry to register their willingness to the release of identifying information to each other by submitting a signed affidavit. The affidavit gives the registry authority to release identifying information related to the registrant to the other relevant persons who register. Each registration shall be accompanied by the birth certificate of the registrant.

A registry shall release only information necessary for identifying a birth parent, adult adopted person, or adult birth sibling and shall not release information of any kind pertaining to the adoptive parents, siblings who are children of the adoptive parents, and the income of anyone.

Any eligible registrant or any adoptive parent may file with the registry an objection to the release of identifying information. When an objection to the release of identifying information has been filed, the court shall hear the objection of the filing party prior to the release of identifying information to determine whether it is in the best interests of the parties to release identifying information.

Access to Original Birth Certificate
Citation: Gen. Laws § 15-7.2-12

In the event of a verified match and release of identifying information, the registry, upon the written request of the adult adopted person, shall certify to the State Registrar of Vital Records that the adult adopted person is a party to a verified match and is entitled to receive uncertified copies of his or her original birth certificate. The certification shall also state that no person other than the adult adopted person is entitled to receive copies of the original birth certificate. However, no uncertified copy of the original birth certificate may be released to the adult adopted person unless each party named on the original birth certificate has registered. Registration by a birth parent not named on the original birth certificate shall not be required for release of the uncertified copy of the original birth certificate.

Where the Information Can Be Located

State of Rhode Island and Providence Plantations Family Court, Voluntary Adoption Reunion Registry

Access to Adoption Records

South Carolina

Who May Access Information
Citation: Ann. Code § 63-9-780
Nonidentifying information may be accessed by the following persons:

- The adoptive parents
- The adopted person
- The birth parents

Identifying information may be accessed by the following persons:

- The adopted person who is age 21 or older
- The birth parents and siblings

Access to Nonidentifying Information
Citation: Ann. Code § 63-9-780
The adoption agency may furnish nonidentifying information to adoptive parents, birth parents, or adopted persons when, in the sole discretion of the chief executive officer of the agency, the information would serve the best interests of the persons concerned. Nonidentifying information includes, but is not limited to, the following:

- The health and medical histories of the birth parents
- The health and medical history of the adopted person
- The adopted person's general family background without name references or geographical designations
- The length of time the adopted person has been in the care and custody of the adoptive parent

Mutual Access to Identifying Information
Citation: Ann. Code § 63-9-780
The public adoption agency responsible for the placement shall furnish to an adopted person the identity of the adopted person's birth parents and siblings, and to the birth parents and siblings the identity of the adopted person under the following conditions:

- The adopted person is age 21 or older, and the applicants apply in writing to the adoption agency for the information.

Child Welfare Information Gateway

- The agency has a current file containing affidavits from the adopted person, the birth parents, and siblings that they are willing to have their identities revealed to each other.
- The agency has established and maintained a confidential register that contains the names and addresses of the adopted person, birth parents, and siblings who have filed affidavits.
- The adopted person and his or her birth parents and siblings have undergone counseling by the adoption agency concerning the effects of the disclosure. The adoption agency may charge a fee for the services, but services must not be denied because of inability to pay.

No disclosure may be made within 30 days after compliance with these conditions. The director of the adoption agency may waive the 30-day period in extreme circumstances. The agency may delay disclosure for 20 days from the expiration of the 30-day period to allow time to apply to a court of competent jurisdiction to enjoin the disclosure for good cause shown.

Access to Original Birth Certificate
Citation: Ann. Code § 44-63-140
The original birth certificate is placed in a special sealed file by the State Registrar. The statute does not specify a procedure for access to the original certificate.

Where the Information Can Be Located
Adoption Reunion Registry, South Carolina Department of Social Services

South Dakota

Who May Access Information
Citation: Ann. Code §§ 25-6-15.2; 25-6-15.3
Nonidentifying information may be released to:

- The adoptive parent
- The adopted person who is age 18 or older

Identifying information may be released to:

- The adopted person
- The birth parents

Access to Adoption Records

Access to Nonidentifying Information
Citation: Ann. Code § 25-6-15.2
Nonidentifying information, if known, shall be made available to the adoptive parent or to the adopted person who is age 18 or older upon written request and proper proof of identification. Information may be withheld only if would tend to identify a birth relative. Nonidentifying information includes:

- The age of the birth parents at the time of the child's birth
- The heritage of the birth parents, including nationality, ethnic background, and race
- The number of years of school completed by the birth parents at the time of the child's birth
- The general physical appearance of the birth parents at the time of the child's birth in terms of height, weight, color of hair, eyes, skin, and other information of a similar nature
- The talents, hobbies, and special interests of the birth parents
- The existence of any other children born to either birth parent before the child's birth
- Whether the termination of parental rights was voluntary or involuntary
- The religion of the birth parents
- The occupations of the birth parents in general terms
- The health history of the birth parents and blood relatives
- The relationship between the birth parents

Mutual Access to Identifying Information
Citation: Ann. Code § 25-6-15.3
The Department of Social Services shall maintain a voluntary registry of adopted persons and birth parents who have presented a consent regarding the release of identifying information about themselves. Any consent shall indicate to whom the information may be released and whether the adopted person desires release of this identifying information after his or her death. A person who uses this voluntary register may revoke his or her consent at any time.

Access to Original Birth Certificate
Citation: Ann. Code § 34-25-16.4
The original birth certificate is available upon order of the court.

Where the Information Can Be Located
South Dakota Department of Social Services, Adoption Registry

Tennessee

Who May Access Information
Citation: Ann. Code §§ 36-1-127; 36-1-128; 36-1-133
Nonidentifying information may be released to:

- The adopted person who is age 18 or older
- The adoptive parents or guardian if the adopted person is under age 18
- The birth parent or legal relatives
- The lineal descendants of an adopted person
- The legal representative of any of the above persons

Identifying information is accessible to the following persons:

- An adopted person who is age 21 or older
- A birth parent or birth sibling
- The spouse, lineal ancestor, or lineal descendant of an adopted person
- The legal representative of any person listed above

Access to Nonidentifying Information
Citation: Ann. Code § 36-1-133
To provide full disclosure about a child to be adopted from the guardianship of the Department of Children's Services, the department shall provide to the adoptive family the following categories of information, to the extent that they are available:

- Historical and current health, mental health, and behavioral health information
- Historical and current educational information
- Nationality, ethnic background, race, and religious preference
- Other information required for the adoptive family to evaluate its ability to provide appropriate care for the child, including daily routine, social and emotional well-being, and personality
- Relevant information about the child's experience in foster care and reasons for coming into care
- Pertinent prenatal and birth information, including birth date, time of birth, weight, and other physical characteristics at birth

Access to Adoption Records

- A general physical description, including height, weight, hair color, eye color, and any other information related to the child's physical appearance

The department also shall provide the following categories of nonidentifying information about the child's birth or legal family, to the extent that they are available:

- Historical and current health, mental health, and behavioral health information
- Historical and current educational and occupational information
- Nationality, ethnic background, race, and religious preference
- A general physical description, including height, weight, hair color, eye color, and any other information related to the physical appearance of the child's birth or legal family

Nothing in this section shall be construed to authorize or require the release of information that may lead to the discovery of the identity or location of the birth or legal relatives of the child to be adopted.

Mutual Access to Identifying Information
Citation: Ann. Code §§ 36-1-128; 36-1-129

The department shall maintain a contact veto registry for permitting registration of the willingness or unwillingness of the persons listed above for contact with persons eligible to have access to records. The registry shall contain the following information:

- The name of each person who has filed a contact veto or who has given consent for contact
- The address and telephone number of the person
- The date and place of birth of the person, if known
- Any persons whom the person who files a contact veto wishes to exclude from the application of the contact veto
- The name, address, and telephone number of the person requesting contact
- The method of contact, if any, to which the person consents, including contact through one or more third parties
- Any other information that eligible parties wish to release to the other eligible parties

92 Child Welfare Information Gateway

A person eligible to file a contact veto or give consent for contact may notify the department in writing that such person does or does not object to contact being made with such person by any person or group of persons who are eligible to establish contact.

As part of the surrender for adoption, a birth parent or guardian shall indicate whether or not he or she wishes to file a contact veto or give consent for further contact. By filing a contact veto, a person is entitled to notification of any inquiry requesting contact with the filing person.

Access to Original Birth Certificate
Citation: Ann. Code § 36-1-130
The original birth certificate is available to parties who have established their eligibility to have access to adoption records.

Where the Information Can Be Located
Tennessee Department of Children's Services, Advance Notice Registry

Texas

Who May Access Information
Citation: Fam. Code §§ 162.018; 162.406
Nonidentifying information may be provided to:

- The adoptive parents
- The adopted person who is age 18 or older

Identifying information may be accessed by:

- The adopted person who is age 18 or older
- A birth parent
- An alleged father who acknowledges paternity
- A birth sibling who is age 18 or older

Access to Nonidentifying Information
Citation: Fam. Code § 162.018
The adoptive parents are entitled to receive copies of the records and other information relating to the history of the child maintained by the department, licensed child-placing agency, person, or entity placing the child for adoption.

The adoptive parents and the adopted person, after the adopted person is an adult, are entitled to receive copies of the records that have been edited to

Access to Adoption Records

protect the identity of the birth parents and any other person whose identity is confidential and other information relating to the history of the child maintained by the department, licensed child-placing agency, person, or entity placing the child for adoption.

At the time an adoption order is rendered, the court shall provide to the parents of an adopted person information provided by the Bureau of Vital Statistics that describes the functions of the voluntary adoption registry. The licensed child-placing agency shall provide to each of the child's birth parents, as known to the agency, the information when the parent signs an affidavit of relinquishment of parental rights or affidavit of waiver of interest in a child. The information shall include the right of the child or birth parent to refuse to participate in the registry. If the adopted child is age 14 or older, the court shall provide the information to the child.

Mutual Access to Identifying Information
Citation: Fam. Code §§ 162.407; 162.413; 162.414; 162.416

The persons listed above may register with a mutual consent voluntary adoption registry. A registration remains in effect until the 99th anniversary of the date the registration is accepted, unless a shorter period is specified by the applicant or the registration is withdrawn. A registrant may withdraw his or her registration in writing at any time.

The applicant must participate in counseling for not less than 1 hour with a social worker or mental health professional with expertise in postadoption counseling before the release of confidential information.

The administrator shall process each registration in an attempt to match the adopted person, the birth parents, and the birth siblings. The administrator shall determine that there is a match if the adult adopted person and the birth mother, father, or sibling has registered.

When a match has been made, the administrator shall mail a written notice to each registrant:

- Informing the registrant that a match has been made
- Reminding the registrant that he or she may withdraw the registration before disclosures are made, if desired
- Notifying the registrant that before any identifying disclosures are made, he or she must sign a written consent and participate in counseling

Identifying information about a registrant shall be released without the registrant's having consented to disclosure after the match if the registrant is

94 Child Welfare Information Gateway

dead, his or her registration was valid at the time of death, and he or she had in writing specifically authorized the postdeath disclosure. Identifying information about a deceased birth parent may not be released until each surviving child is an adult or until each child's surviving parent or guardian consents in writing to the disclosure.

Access to Original Birth Certificate
Citation: Health & Safety Code § 192.008
Only the court that granted the adoption may grant access to the original birth certificate.

Where the Information Can Be Located
Texas Department of State Health Services, Central Adoption Registry

Utah

Who May Access Information
Citation: Ann. Code §§ 78B-6-143; 78B-6-144
Nonidentifying information is available to:

- The adoptive parents
- The adopted person's legal guardian if the adoptive parents are deceased
- The adopted person
- The adopted person's spouse or guardian of the adopted person's child if the adopted person is deceased
- The adopted person's child or descendant
- The birth parent or adult birth sibling

Identifying information is accessible to:

- The adult adopted person
- Birth parents
- A birth sibling who is age 18 or older

Access to Nonidentifying Information
Citation: Ann. Code § 78B-6-143
A detailed health history and a genetic and social history of the adopted person that is on file with the Office of Vital Records and Statistics shall be available upon request to the persons listed above.

Mutual Access to Identifying Information
Citation: Ann. Code § 78B-6-144

The adult adopted person and birth parents, upon presentation of positive identification, may request identifying information from the adoption registry maintained by the office. The office may release identifying information only when it receives requests from both the adopted person and the birth parent. After matching the request of an adult adopted person with that of at least one birth parent, the office shall notify both the adopted person and the birth parent that the requests have been matched and disclose the identifying information to those parties. However, if the adult adopted person has a sibling of the same birth parent who is under age 18, and who was raised in the same family setting as the adult adopted person, the office may not disclose the requested identifying information to that adult adopted person or the birth parent.

Adult adopted persons and adult siblings, upon presentation of positive identification, may request identifying information from the registry, following the same procedure outlined above.

Information registered with the office is available only to a registered adult adopted person, and his or her registered birth parent or registered adult sibling. The office may not disclose information regarding a birth parent who has not registered a request with the office.

Access to Original Birth Certificate
Citation: Ann. Code §§ 78B-6-103(3); 78B-6-141

An 'adoption document' is an adoption-related document filed with the office, a petition for adoption, a decree of adoption, an original birth certificate, or evidence submitted in support of a supplementary birth certificate.

An adoption document is sealed and may only be open to inspection and copying as follows:

- By a party to the adoption proceeding while the proceeding is pending or within 6 months after the adoption decree is entered
- When a court enters an order permitting access to the documents by a person who has appealed the denial of that person's motion to intervene
- Upon order of the court expressly permitting inspection or copying, after good cause has been shown
- As provided under § 78B-6-144
- When the adoption document becomes public on the 100th anniversary of the date the final decree of adoption was entered

96 Child Welfare Information Gateway

- When the birth certificate becomes public on the 100th anniversary of the date of birth
- To a mature adopted person or a parent who adopted the mature adopted person without a court order, unless the final decree of adoption is entered by the juvenile court
- To an adult adopted person, to the extent permitted below

For an adoption finalized on or after January 1, 2016, a birth parent may elect, on a written consent form provided by the office, to permit identifying information about the birth parent to be made available for inspection by an adult adopted person. A birth parent may, at any time, change the election or elect to make other information about the birth parent, including an updated medical history, available for inspection by an adult adopted person.

A birth parent may not access any identifying information or an adoption document under this subsection.

Where the Information Can Be Located

Utah Department of Administrative Services, Division of Archives and Record Service, Adoption Records

Vermont

Who May Access Information
Citation: Ann. Stat. Tit. 15A, §§ 6-104; 6-105
Nonidentifying information is available to:

- The adoptive parent or legal guardian of an adopted person
- The adopted person who is age 18 or older or has been emancipated
- A deceased adopted person's direct descendant who is age 18 or older, or a parent or guardian of a descendant who is under age 18
- The adopted person's birth parent, grandparent, or sibling

Identifying information may be disclosed to:

- An adopted person who is age 18 or older or has been emancipated
- A deceased adopted person's direct descendant who is age 18 or older or the parent or guardian of a direct descendant who is younger than age 18
- The birth parent
- A birth sibling who is age 18 or older

Access to Adoption Records

Access to Nonidentifying Information
Citation: Ann. Stat. Tit. 15A, §§ 6-104; 2-105

Any person listed above may request a detailed summary of any relevant report about the adopted person, the birth parents, and the adopted person's genetic history, including the information required by § 2-105 of this title. This report shall exclude identifying information concerning an individual who has not signed a waiver of confidentiality. The report shall include all of the following nonidentifying information that is reasonably available:

- A social and health history of the child
- Any physical, sexual, or emotional abuse known to have been experienced by the child
- Enrollment and performance in school, results of educational testing, and any special educational needs
- An account of the child's past and existing relationships with any relative, foster parent, or other persons
- A social and health history of the minor's parents and extended family, including:
  - Health and genetic history, including any known hereditary condition or disease
  - Racial, ethnic, and religious background and general physical description
  - Educational, vocational, athletic, artistic, or scientific achievement or interests
  - The existence of any other child of the parents

Mutual Access to Identifying Information
Citation: Ann. Stat. Tit. 15A, §§ 6-105; 6-106

For adoptions finalized prior to July 1, 1986, the registry shall disclose identifying information if the birth parent has filed any kind of document that clearly indicates that he or she consents to such disclosure.

For adoptions finalized on or after July 1, 1986, the registry shall disclose identifying information without requiring the consent of the birth parent unless the birth parent has filed a request for nondisclosure in accordance with the provisions of § 6-106 of this title and has not withdrawn the request.

Identifying information about the adopted person shall be disclosed to the birth parent if the adoptive parent of the adopted person who is younger than age 18 consents to the disclosure. Identifying information about a deceased

98 Child Welfare Information Gateway

adopted person shall be disclosed to the birth parent or sibling upon request if the deceased adopted person's direct descendant is age 18 or older and consents to the disclosure, or the parent or guardian of a direct descendant who is younger than age 18 consents to the disclosure. Identifying information about a birth sibling shall be disclosed to the adopted person upon request if both the sibling and the adopted person are age 18 or older and the sibling consents to disclosure.

A birth parent may prevent disclosure of identifying information by filing a request for nondisclosure with the registry. A request for nondisclosure may be withdrawn by a birth parent at any time.

Access to Original Birth Certificate
Citation: Ann. Stat. Tit. 15A, § 6-107
The original birth certificate may be released upon request to an adopted person who is age 18 or older and who has access to identifying information.

The original birth certificate is unsealed and becomes public record 99 years after the date of the adopted person's birth.

Where the Information Can Be Located
Vermont Adoption Registry, Department for Children and Families

Virgin Islands

Who May Access Information
Citation: Ann. Code Tit. 16, § 145
The adult adopted person may access information.

Access to Nonidentifying Information
This issue is not addressed in the statutes reviewed.

Mutual Access to Identifying Information
Citation: Ann. Code Tit. 16, § 145
All records and files are sealed and are not available to anyone other than the adopted person upon attaining majority or upon order of the court.

Access to Original Birth Certificate
Citation: Ann. Code Tit. 16, § 145
The original birth record is not available to anyone other than the adopted person after attaining majority or upon order of the court.

Where the Information Can Be Located
This issue is not addressed in the statutes reviewed.

Virginia

Who May Access Information
Citation: Ann. Code §§ 63.2-1246; 63.2-1247
Nonidentifying information may be disclosed to:

- The adopted person who is age 18 or older
- The licensed or authorized child-placing agencies providing services to the child
- The adoptive parents

Identifying information may be released to:

- The adopted person who is age 21 or older
- The birth parents
- An adult birth sibling

Access to Nonidentifying Information
Citation: Ann. Code § 63.2-1246
Nonidentifying information shall not be open to inspection or be copied by anyone other than those listed above, except upon the order of a circuit court upon good cause shown.

Mutual Access to Identifying Information
Citation: Ann. Code § 63.2-1247
For adoptions finalized on or after July 1, 1994, the following requests for disclosure of identifying information are permitted in the following circumstances:

- The adopted person who is age 21 or older may apply for information about the birth family.
- The birth parents and adult birth siblings may apply for information about the adopted person.
- When the adopted person is under age 18, the adoptive parents or other legal custodian of the child may apply for information about the birth family.

The Commissioner of Social Services shall designate the person or agency that prepared the home study to attempt to locate and advise the person whose information is sought of the application. The designated person or agency shall report the results of the attempt to locate and advise the adopted person to the commissioner, including the effects that disclosure of the identifying information may have on the adopted person, the adoptive parents, and the birth family. The adopted person and the birth family may submit to the commissioner, and the commissioner shall consider, written comments stating the effect that the disclosure of identifying information may have upon any party. Upon a showing of good cause, the commissioner shall disclose the identifying information. When consent of the person being sought is not obtainable due to death or mental incapacity, the circuit court may release identifying information to the person making the request. In making this decision, the circuit court shall consider the needs and concerns of all persons involved.

In parental placement adoptions, where the consent to the adoption was executed on or after July 1, 1994, the entire adoption record shall be open to the adoptive parents, the adopted person who is age 18 or older, and the birth parent who executed a written consent.

Access to Original Birth Certificate
Citation: Ann. Code § 32.1-261
Upon receipt of notice of a decision or order granting an adult adopted person access to identifying information regarding his or her birth parents from the Commissioner of Social Services or a circuit court, and proof of identification and payment, the State Registrar shall mail an adult adopted person a copy of the original certificate of birth.

Where the Information Can Be Located
Virginia Department of Social Services, Adoption Unit

Washington

Who May Access Information
Citation: Rev. Code §§ 26.33.340; 26.33.343
Nonidentifying information is available to:

- An adoptive parent
- An adopted person
- A birth parent

Identifying information may be accessed by:

Access to Adoption Records 101

- An adopted person who is age 21 or older, or under 21 with the permission of the adoptive parent
- A birth parent or member of the birth parent's family after the adopted person has reached age 21

These family members shall be limited to the birth grandparents, a brother or sister of a birth parent, or the child of a birth parent. The court, for good cause shown, may allow a relative more distant in degree to petition for disclosure.

Access to Nonidentifying Information
Citation: Rev. Code §§ 26.33.340; 26.33.380

Reasonably available nonidentifying information may be disclosed upon a written request to the persons listed above. If the adoption facilitator refuses to disclose such information, the individual may petition the superior court.

The prospective adoptive parent shall be given a family background and child and family social history report about the child. The report shall include a chronological history of the circumstances surrounding the adoptive placement and any available psychiatric reports, psychological reports, court reports pertaining to dependency or custody, or school reports. Such reports or information shall not reveal the identity of the birth parents of the child but shall contain reasonably available nonidentifying information.

Mutual Access to Identifying Information
Citation: Rev. Code §§ 26.33.343; 26.33.347

Any person listed above may petition the court to appoint a confidential intermediary. The intermediary shall search for and discreetly contact the birth parent or adopted person; or if they are not alive or cannot be located within 1 year, the intermediary may attempt to locate members of the birth parents' or adopted person's family.

If the person is located, the intermediary will ask whether the person consents to a disclosure of identifying information. If the person refuses to consent, the intermediary shall report the refusal to the court and shall refrain from further inquiry without judicial approval. If the person being sought consents to disclosure of his or her identity, the court may then order that the identifying information be released. If the person being sought is deceased, the court may order disclosure of the identity of the deceased to the petitioner.

An adopted person age 18 or older may file with the Department of Health a certified statement declaring any one or more of the following:

- The adopted person refuses to consent to the release of any identifying information to a birth parent, birth sibling, or other birth relative and does not wish to be contacted by a confidential intermediary except in the case of a medical need.
- The adopted person consents to the release of identifying information to a confidential intermediary, a birth parent, birth sibling, or other birth relative.
- The adopted person desires to be contacted by his or her birth parents, birth siblings, other birth relatives, or a confidential intermediary.

An adopted person who files a certified statement may subsequently file another statement requesting to rescind or amend the prior statement.

Access to Original Birth Certificate
Citation: Rev. Code § 26.33.345

A noncertified copy of the original birth certificate is available to the birth parent upon request.

For adoptions finalized after October 1, 1993, the Department of Health shall provide a noncertified copy of the original birth certificate upon request to an adopted person who is age 18 or older, unless the birth parent has filed an affidavit of nondisclosure before July 28, 2013, or a contact preference form that indicates he or she does not want the original birth certificate released, provided that the affidavit of nondisclosure, the contact preference form, or both have not expired.

For adoptions finalized on or before October 1, 1993, the department may not provide a noncertified copy of the original birth certificate to the adopted person until after June 30, 2014. After June 30, 2014, the department shall provide a noncertified copy of the original birth certificate upon request to an adopted person age 18 or older, unless the birth parent has filed a contact preference form that indicates he or she does not want the original birth certificate released, provided that the contact preference form has not expired.

An affidavit of nondisclosure expires upon the death of the birth parent.

Where the Information Can Be Located

Washington State Department Health, Original Birth Certificate for an Adopted Person

Access to Adoption Records

West Virginia

Who May Access Information
Citation: Ann. Code §§ 48-23-601; 48-23-402
Nonidentifying information may be provided to:

- The adoptive parents or, in the event of death of the adoptive parents, the child's guardian
- The adopted person who is age 18 or older
- The birth parent

If the adopted person is deceased, nonidentifying information may be provided to:

- The adopted person's spouse if he or she is the legal parent of the adopted person's child or the guardian of any child of the adopted person
- Any progeny of the adopted person who is age 18 or older

Identifying information may be obtained through the mutual consent voluntary adoption registry by:

- The birth parent when the child is age 18 or older
- The adult adopted person except when there is a sibling in his or her adoptive family who is under age 18

Access to Nonidentifying Information
Citation: Ann. Code § 48-23-601
Prior to placement for adoption, the agency shall compile and provide to the prospective adoptive parents a detailed written health history and genetic and social history of the child. These histories must exclude information that would identify birth parents or members of a birth parent's family.

Records containing such nonidentifying information shall be retained by the clerk of the court for 99 years, and shall be available upon request, together with any additional nonidentifying information that may have been added on health or genetic and social history, to any person listed above.

Mutual Access to Identifying Information
Citation: Ann. Code §§ 48-23-501 through 48-23-504; 48-22-702

104   Child Welfare Information Gateway

The adult adopted person and each birth parent may register by submitting an affidavit to the registry. The failure of any person to file with the registry for any reason, including death or disability, precludes the disclosure of identifying information to those persons who do register.

Upon registering, the registrant must participate in no less than 1 hour of counseling with a social worker.

In any case where the identity of the birth father was unknown to the birth mother, or one or both of the birth parents are deceased, this information shall be shared with the adult adopted person. In these cases, the adopted person will not be able to obtain identifying information through the registry.

The affidavit must include, if known:

- The current name and address and any previous name by which the person was known
- The child's original and adopted names
- The place and date of the child's birth
- The name and address of the agency that placed the child

The administrator of the registry shall process each affidavit in an attempt to match the adopted person and the birth parents. There is a match when the adult adopted person and the birth parent have each registered and received the required counseling. When a match has taken place, the department shall directly notify all parties through a direct and confidential contact.

If an adopted person or a parent of a minor adopted person cannot obtain identifying information by use of the registry, identifying information may be sought by petitioning the court. If the court is unable to obtain consent from either of the birth parents, the court may release identifying information to the adopted person if at a hearing the court finds there is evidence of compelling medical or other good cause for release of such identifying information.

Access to Original Birth Certificate
Citation: Ann. Code § 16-5-18

The State Registrar shall establish a new certificate of birth for a person born in West Virginia when he or she receives a certificate of adoption or a certified copy of the order of adoption, together with the information necessary to identify the original certificate of birth and to establish a new certificate of birth.

A new certificate of birth shall show the actual city, county and date of birth, if known, and shall be substituted for the original certificate of birth on file. The original certificate of birth and the evidence of adoption may be inspected only upon order of a court of competent jurisdiction, except as provided by legislative rule or as otherwise provided by State law.

Where the Information Can Be Located
West Virginia Mutual Consent Voluntary Adoption Registry, Department of Health and Human Resources

Wisconsin

Who May Access Information
Citation: Ann. Stat. §§ 48.432; 48.433
Nonidentifying information may be provided to:

- The adopted person who is age 18 years or older
- The adoptive parent
- The guardian or legal custodian of an adopted person
- The offspring of an adopted person if the requester is age 18 or older
- An agency or social worker assigned to provide services to the adopted person or place the child for adoption

Identifying information may be accessed by the adopted person who is age 21 or older.

Access to Nonidentifying Information
Citation: Ann. Stat. §§ 48.432; 48.433
Whenever any person listed above wishes to obtain medical and genetic information about a birth parent who consented to his or her child's adoption before February 1, 1982, and the information is not on file with the department or agency, the person may request that the department or agency conduct a search for the birth parents to obtain the information. The request shall be accompanied by a statement from a physician certifying either that the individual has or may have acquired a genetically transferable disease or that the individual's medical condition requires access to the information.

If a birth parent is located but refuses to provide the information requested, the department or agency shall notify the requester without disclosing the birth parents identity or location, and the requester may petition the circuit court to order the birth parent to disclose the information. If the department or another agency that maintains records relating to the adoption

106 Child Welfare Information Gateway

receives a report from a physician stating that a birth parent or another offspring of the birth parent has acquired or may have a genetically transferable disease, the department or agency shall notify the adopted person

of the existence of the disease, if he or she is age 18 or older, or notify the adopted person's guardian or adoptive parent if he or she is younger than age 18.

If the department or agency may not disclose the identifying information requested per § 48.433, it shall provide the requester with any nonidentifying social history information about either of the birth parents that it has on file.

Mutual Access to Identifying Information
Citation: Ann. Stat. § 48.433

The birth parent may file an affidavit authorizing the release of any available information about the birth parent's identity and location. An affidavit may be revoked at any time by notifying the department or agency in writing.

An adopted person who is age 21 or older may request any available information regarding the identity and location of his or her birth parents. The requested information may be disclosed if the department or agency has on file unrevoked affidavits from both birth parents, or if one of the birth parents was unknown and the known birth parent has filed an unrevoked affidavit.

If the department or agency does not have on file an affidavit from each known birth parent, it shall, within 3 months after the date of the original request, search for each birth parent who has not filed an affidavit. If the birth parent is contacted and files an affidavit, the department shall disclose the requested information. If the birth parent does not file the affidavit, the department may not disclose the information. If, after a search, a known birth parent cannot be located, the department may disclose the requested information if the other birth parent has filed an unrevoked affidavit.

If a birth parent is known to be dead and has not filed an unrevoked affidavit, the department shall so inform the requester. The department may not release the identity of that parent but shall release any available information regarding the identity and location of the other birth parent, if the other birth parent has filed an unrevoked affidavit and 1 year has elapsed since the death of the deceased birth parent.

The requester may petition the court to order the release of any information that may not be disclosed under this section.

Access to Original Birth Certificate
Citation: Ann. Stat. § 48.433

The original birth certificate is available upon request to the adopted person who is age 21 or older if the birth parents have filed affidavits authorizing disclosure.

Where the Information Can Be Located
Adoption Records Search Program, Wisconsin Department of Children and Families

Wyoming

Who May Access Information
Citation: Ann. Stat. §§ 1-22-116; 1-22-203
Nonidentifying medical information may be provided to:

- The adoptive parent
- The adult adopted person

Identifying information may be accessed by:

- The adult adopted person
- The adoptive parent
- The birth parent, sibling, or grandparent

All parties must be age 18 or older.
Access to Nonidentifying Information
Citation: Ann. Stat. § 1-22-116
To the extent available, the medical history of the adoptive child and his or her birth parents, with information identifying the birth parents eliminated, shall be provided to the child's adoptive parent any time after the adoption decree or to the child after he or she attains the age of majority. The history shall include but not be limited to all available information regarding conditions or diseases believed to be hereditary, any drugs or medication taken during pregnancy by the birth mother, and any other information that may be a factor influencing the child's present or future health.
Mutual Access to Identifying Information
Citation: Ann. Stat. § 1-22-203
Any person listed above may petition the court to appoint one or more confidential intermediaries for the purpose of determining the whereabouts of

an unknown birth relative, except that no one shall seek a relative who is a minor. Any information obtained by the intermediary shall be kept strictly confidential and shall be utilized only for the purpose of arranging a contact between the individual who initiated the search and the sought-after birth relative.

When a sought-after relative is located:

- Contact shall be made between the parties only when written consent for such contact has been obtained from both parties and filed with the court.
- If consent for personal communication is not obtained from both parties, all relinquishment and adoption records and any information obtained by any confidential intermediary during the course of his or her investigation shall be returned to the court and shall remain confidential.

Access to Original Birth Certificate
Citation: Ann. Stat. § 35-1-417
The original birth certificate is not subject to inspection except by court order.
Where the Information Can Be Located
Wyoming Department of Family Services, Adoption

End Notes

[1] Idaho, Nevada, and New Jersey provide nonidentifying medical and social information about the birth family to adopting parents at the time of placement, but do not otherwise address the issue of access to nonidentifying information in statute.

[2] The word "approximately" is used to stress the fact that the States frequently amend their laws. This information is current through June 2015. The States that allow birth parents access to nonidentifying information are Alabama, Arizona, Arkansas, Connecticut, Delaware, Louisiana, Maryland, Massachusetts, Michigan, Mississippi, Montana, New Hampshire, New Mexico, New York, North Dakota, Ohio, Oklahoma, Oregon, Pennsylvania (if the adopted person is at least age 21), Rhode Island, South Carolina, Tennessee, Utah, Vermont, Washington, and West Virginia.

[3] Arizona, Colorado, Michigan, Mississippi, Montana, New Mexico, New York, North Carolina, Ohio, Oklahoma, Pennsylvania, Rhode Island, Tennessee, Utah, and Vermont.

[4] New Jersey, the District of Columbia, American Samoa, and Guam require a court order for release of identifying information. The Virgin Islands requires a court order for release of information to any person other than the adult adopted person. Statutes in Puerto Rico require a court order for release of any information from the adoption records to interested parties.

Access to Adoption Records   109

[5] A compelling reason might include, for example, a serious medical condition requiring a blood relative or genetic link, or access to medical records.

[6] Arizona, Arkansas, California, Colorado, Connecticut, Florida, Georgia, Idaho, Illinois, Iowa, Kentucky, Louisiana, Maine, Maryland, Michigan, Minnesota, Missouri, Montana, Nevada, New Hampshire, New Mexico, New York, North Carolina, North Dakota, Ohio, Oklahoma, Oregon, Pennsylvania, Rhode Island, South Carolina, Tennessee, Texas, Utah, Vermont, Virginia, Washington, and Wyoming.

[7] See Connecticut Gen. Stat. § 45a-751.

[8] Arizona, Arkansas, Delaware, Florida, Georgia, Hawaii, Idaho, Illinois, Indiana, Iowa, Louisiana, Maine, Maryland, Michigan, Missouri, Nevada, New Hampshire, New York, Ohio, Oklahoma, Oregon, Pennsylvania, Rhode Island, South Carolina, South Dakota, Tennessee, Texas, Utah, Vermont, and West Virginia.

[9] The States that will release identifying information unless a nonconsent form has been filed are Hawaii, Indiana (for adoptions finalized after 12/31/1993), Maryland (for adoptions finalized after 1/1/2000), Michigan (for adoptions finalized before 5/28/1948 or after 9/12/1980), Minnesota (for adoptions finalized after 8/1/1982), Nebraska (for adoptions finalized after 9/1/1998), Ohio (for adoptions finalized after 1996), and Vermont (for adoptions finalized after 7/1/1986).

[10] States using confidential intermediaries include Alabama (when consent is not on file), Colorado, Florida (to contact family members who have not registered with the adoption registry), Illinois (to obtain updated medical information), Michigan (when consent is not on file), Montana, North Carolina, North Dakota, Oklahoma, Virginia, Washington, and Wyoming.

[11] Alabama, Alaska, California, Kentucky, Massachusetts, Minnesota, Mississippi, Nebraska, New Hampshire, New Mexico, Pennsylvania, and Wisconsin.

[12] Arizona, Arkansas, California, Florida, Georgia, Hawaii, Iowa, Kansas, Kentucky, Louisiana, Massachusetts, Missouri, Montana (for adoptions finalized on or after 10/1/1985 and before 10/1/1997), Nevada, New Hampshire, New Jersey (until 1/1/2017), New Mexico, New York, North Carolina, North Dakota, South Carolina, South Dakota, Texas, West Virginia, and Wyoming.

[13] Idaho, Mississippi, and the Northern Mariana Islands.

[14] Alabama, Alaska, Connecticut (for adoptions finalized on or after 10/1/1983), Illinois (for adopted persons born prior to 1/1/1946), Maine, Montana (for adoptions finalized before 10/1/1985), New Jersey (effective 1/1/2017), Oregon, and the Virgin Islands.

[15] Colorado (effective 1/1/2016), Delaware, Illinois (for adopted persons born on or after 1/1/1946), Maryland (for adoptions finalized on or after 1/1/2000), Minnesota (for adoptions finalized on or after 8/1/1997), Montana (for adoptions finalized on or after 10/1/1997), Nebraska (for adoptions finalized on or after 7/20/2002), Ohio (for adoptions finalized after 1996), Oklahoma (for adoptions finalized on or after 11/1/1997 when there are no birth siblings under age 18 who have been adopted), and Washington.

[16] Indiana (for adoptions finalized after 12/31/1993), Michigan, Rhode Island, Tennessee, Utah, Vermont, and Virginia.

[17] Nebraska (for adoptions finalized on or after 9/1/1998), Pennsylvania, Utah (for adoptions finalized on or after 1/1/2016), and Wisconsin.

In: Adoption Records …
Editor: Ebony Bartlett

ISBN: 978-1-63485-437-5
© 2016 Nova Science Publishers, Inc.

Chapter 2

POSTADOPTION CONTACT AGREEMENTS BETWEEN BIRTH AND ADOPTIVE FAMILIES[*]

Child Welfare Information Gateway

Postadoption contact agreements are arrangements that allow contact between a child's adoptive family and members of the child's birth family or other persons with whom the child has an established relationship, such as a foster parent, after the child's adoption has been finalized. These arrangements, sometimes referred to as cooperative adoption or open adoption agreements, can range from informal, mutual understandings between the birth and adoptive families to written, formal contracts.

Agreements for postadoption contact or communication have become more prevalent in recent years due to several factors:

- There is wider recognition of the rights of birth parents to make choices for their children.
- Many adoptions involve older children, such as stepchildren and children adopted from foster care; these children frequently have attachments to one or more birth relatives with whom ongoing contact may be desirable and beneficial.

---

[*] This is an edited, reformatted and augmented version of a document issued by the U.S. Department of Health and Human Services, Children's Bureau, 2014. State statute summaries are current through June 2014.

- Birth parents who participate in selecting the adoptive family may have a wide range of adoptive parent choices and may base their selection on the willingness of the adoptive parent(s) to allow postadoption contact.
- Contact or communication with birth relatives can be a resource to adoptive parents for information about their child's medical, social, and cultural histories.[1]

WHAT'S INSIDE

States with enforceable contact agreements
Who may be a party to an agreement?
The court's role in establishing and enforcing agreements standards for making a report
When do States use mediation?
Laws in States without enforceable agreements
Summaries of State laws
To find statute information for a particular State, go to
https://www.childwelfare. gov/systemwide/ laws_policies/state/

STATES WITH ENFORCEABLE CONTACT AGREEMENTS

In general, State law does not prohibit postadoption contact or communication. Because adoptive parents have the right to decide who may have contact with their adopted child, they can allow any amount of contact with birth family members, and such contacts often are arranged by mutual understanding without any formal agreement.

A written contractual agreement between the parties to an adoption can clarify the type and frequency of the contact or communication and can provide a way for the agreement to be legally enforced. Approximately 28 States and the District of Columbia currently have statutes that allow written and enforceable agreements for contact after the finalization of an adoption.[2] The written agreements specify the type and frequency of contact and are signed by the parties to an adoption prior to finalization.[3]

Contact can range from the adoptive and birth parents exchanging information about a child (e.g., cards, letters, and photos via traditional or social media) to the child exchanging information or having visits with the birth parents or relatives.

Who May Be a Party to an Agreement?

In most States that permit enforceable agreements, an agreement for contact after adoption is permitted for any adoptive child as long as the nature and frequency of contact are deemed by the court to be in the child's best interests and are designed to protect the safety of the child and the rights of all the parties to the agreement. Some States limit the enforceability of such agreements based on factors such as the type of adoption, the age of the adoptive child, or the nature of the contact. For example, Connecticut, Nebraska, and Utah limit agreements to children who have been adopted from foster care. Wisconsin limits such agreements to adoptions by stepparents and relatives. Indiana limits enforceable contact agreements to children ages 2 and older. For children under age 2, nonenforceable agreements are permitted as long as the type of contact does not include visitation. Oklahoma allows postadoption visitation by a birth relative only when the child has resided with the relative prior to adoption.

Most statutes permit postadoption contact or communication for birth parents. Some States also allow other birth relatives who have significant emotional ties to the child to be included in the agreement, including grandparents, aunts, uncles, and siblings. Minnesota permits former foster parents to petition for contact privileges. In California, Minnesota, and Oklahoma, when the case involves an Indian child, members of the child's Tribe are included among the eligible birth relatives. In 12 States, visits between siblings who have been separated by the adoption may be included in an agreement.[4]

The Court's Role in Establishing and Enforcing Agreements

For the agreements to be enforceable, they must be approved by the court that has jurisdiction over the adoption. Generally, all parties to be included in the agreement must agree in writing to all terms of the agreement prior to the adoption finalization. The court may approve the agreement only if all parties

114 Child Welfare Information Gateway

agree on its provisions, and the court finds the agreement is in the best interests of the child. In Arizona and Louisiana, the court must obtain and consider the wishes of the child if he or she is age 12 or older. In New Mexico, the court must consider the wishes of a child who is age 14 or older. Seven States require the written consent of the adoptive child who is age 12 or older.[5] In six States and the District of Columbia, consent must be obtained from the adoptive child if he or she is age 14 or older.[6]

Disputes over compliance and requests for modification of the terms also must be brought before the court. Any party to the agreement may petition the court to modify, order compliance with, or void the agreement. The court may do so only if the parties agree or circumstances have changed, and the action is determined to be in the best interests of the child.

WHEN DO STATES USE MEDIATION?

Nine States and the District of Columbia require the parties to participate or attempt to participate in mediation before petitions for enforcement or modification of an agreement are brought before the court.[7] New Hampshire law provides for postadoption contact agreements to be negotiated through a voluntary court-approved mediation program. In Florida, Georgia, and Maryland, the court, at its discretion, may refer the parties to mediation. In Massachusetts, any party seeking to enforce an agreement may voluntarily choose mediation. In no case can disputes over the postadoption agreement be used as grounds for setting aside an adoption or relinquishment of parental rights.

LAWS IN STATES WITHOUT ENFORCEABLE AGREEMENTS

In most States without enforceable agreements, the statutes are silent about the issue of postadoption contact or communication. Approximately six other States address the issue but do not provide for enforceable agreements:

- North Carolina's statute, while providing that such agreements may be entered into by a person giving adoption consent and a prospective adoptive parent, specifically states that contracts are not enforceable and cannot be a condition for consent to the adoption.

Postadoption Contact Agreements between Birth and Adoptive ... 115

- Ohio, South Carolina, and South Dakota specifically state that mutual agreements for contact are nonbinding and nonenforceable.
- Missouri and Tennessee leave decisions about contact and visitation with birth relatives to the sole discretion of the adoptive parents.

> This publication is a product of the State Statutes Series prepared by Child Welfare Information Gateway. While every attempt has been made to be complete, additional information on these topics may be in other sections of a State's code as well as agency regulations, case law, and informal practices and procedures.

Alabama

What may be included in postadoption contact agreements?
Ann. Code § 26-10A-30
Postadoption visitation rights may be granted to the natural grandparents of the adopted child.

Who may be a party to a postadoption contact agreement?
Ann. Code § 26-10A-30
Postadoption visitation rights for the natural grandparents of the adopted child may be granted when the child is adopted by a stepparent, a grandfather, a grandmother, a brother, a half-brother, a sister, a half-sister, an aunt, or an uncle and their respective spouses, if any.

What is the role of the court in postadoption contact agreements?
Ann. Code § 26-10A-30
Such visitation rights may be maintained or granted at the discretion of the court at any time prior to or after the final order of adoption is entered upon petition by the natural grandparents, if it is in the best interests of the child.

Are agreements legally enforceable?
This issue is not addressed in the statutes reviewed.

How may an agreement be terminated or modified?
This issue is not addressed in the statutes reviewed.

Alaska

What may be included in postadoption contact agreements?
Alaska Stat. §§ 25.23.130(c); 47.10.089(d)
Nothing in this chapter prohibits an adoption that allows visitation between the adopted child and the adopted child's natural parents or other relatives.

A parent may retain privileges with respect to the child, including the ability to have future contact, communication, and visitation with the child in a voluntary relinquishment to the Department of Health and Social Services. A retained privilege must be in writing and stated with specificity.

Who may be a party to a postadoption contact agreement?
Alaska Stat. §§ 25.23.130(c); 47.10.089(d)
The adopted child and the adopted child's natural parents or other relatives may participate.

What is the role of the court in postadoption contact agreements?
Alaska Stat. §§ 25.23.180(j); 47.10.089(e)
In a relinquishment of parental rights, a parent may retain privileges with respect to the child, such as the ability to have future contact, communication, and visitation, if the privilege is stated in writing with specificity. If the parent has retained privileges, the court shall incorporate the retained privileges into the termination order with a recommendation that the privileges retained be incorporated in an adoption decree.

Are agreements legally enforceable?
Alaska Stat. §§ 25.23.180(k), (l); 47.10.089(f)&(g)
A voluntary relinquishment may not be withdrawn and a termination order may not be vacated on the grounds that a retained privilege has been withheld from the relinquishing parent or that the relinquishing parent has been unable, for any reason, to act on a retained privilege.

Upon a showing of good cause, a person who has voluntarily relinquished parental rights may request a review hearing to seek enforcement.

How may an agreement be terminated or modified?
Alaska Stat. §§ 25.23.180(l); 47.10.089(g)&(j)
Upon a showing of good cause, a person who has voluntarily relinquished parental rights may request a review hearing to seek enforcement or modification of or to vacate a privilege retained in the termination order. The court may modify, enforce, or vacate the privilege if doing so would, by clear and convincing evidence, be in the best interests of the child.

After a termination order is entered and before the entry of an adoption decree, the prospective adoptive parent may request that the court decline to incorporate a privilege retained in a termination order and recommended for incorporation in an adoption decree. The court may decline to incorporate a retained privilege if the person who retained the privilege agrees with the request or if the court finds that it is in the child's best interests.

American Samoa

These issues are not addressed in the statutes reviewed.

Arizona

What may be included in postadoption contact agreements?
Rev. Stat. Ann. § 8-116.01
The parties to a proceeding under this chapter may enter into an agreement regarding communication with an adopted child, the adoptive parents, and a birth parent.

The agreement shall state that the adoptive parent may terminate contact between the birth parent and the adopted child at any time if the adoptive parent believes that this contact is not in the child's best interests.

The agreement shall contain a clause stating that the parties agree to the continuing jurisdiction of the court to enforce and modify the agreement and that they understand that failure to comply with the agreement is not grounds for setting aside an adoption decree or for revocation of a written consent to an adoption or relinquishment of parental rights.

Who may be a party to a postadoption contact agreement?
Rev. Stat. Ann. § 8-116.01
The court shall not approve an agreement unless the agreement is approved by the prospective adoptive parents, any birth parent with whom the agreement is being made, and if the child is in the custody of the division or an agency, a representative of the division or agency.

What is the role of the court in postadoption contact agreements?
Rev. Stat. Ann. § 8-116.01
The court shall not approve the agreement unless the court finds that the communication between the adopted child, the adoptive parents, and a birth

parent is in the child's best interests. The court may consider the wishes of a child who is at least 12 years old.

The court retains jurisdiction after the decree of adoption is entered to hear motions brought to enforce or modify an order entered pursuant to this section. Before filing a motion, the party seeking to enforce or modify an order shall make a good faith attempt to mediate the dispute. The court shall not enforce or modify an order unless the party filing the motion has made a good faith attempt to mediate the dispute.

Are agreements legally enforceable?
Rev. Stat. Ann. § 8-116.01

An agreement is not enforceable unless the agreement is in writing and is approved by the court.

An agreement entered into pursuant to this section is enforceable even if it does not disclose the identity of the parties to the agreement.

Failure to comply with an agreement is not grounds for setting aside an adoption decree or for revocation of a written consent to an adoption or relinquishment of parental rights.

How may an agreement be terminated or modified?
Rev. Stat. Ann. § 8-116.01

The court may order a modification of an agreement if it finds that the modification is necessary to serve the best interests of the adopted child, and one of the following is true:

- The modification is agreed to by the adoptive parents.
- Exceptional circumstances have arisen since the agreement was approved that justify modification of the agreement.

The court may consider the wishes of a child who is at least age 12 in determining whether to order a modification.

Arkansas

These issues are not addressed in the statutes reviewed.

California

What may be included in postadoption contact agreements?
Fam. Code § 8616.5; Welf. & Inst. Code § 366.29
The terms of any postadoption contact agreement shall be limited to, but need not include, all of the following:

- Provisions for visitation between the child and a birth parent or parents and other birth relatives, including siblings, and the child's Indian Tribe if the case is governed by the Indian Child Welfare Act
- Provisions for future contact between a birth parent or parents or other birth relatives, including siblings, or both, and the child or an adoptive parent, or both, and in cases governed by the Indian Child Welfare Act, the child's Indian Tribe
- Provisions for the sharing of information about the child in the future

The terms of any postadoption contact agreement shall be limited to the sharing of information about the child unless the child has an existing relationship with the birth relative.

A postadoption agreement shall contain the following warnings in bold type:

- After the adoption petition has been granted by the court, the adoption cannot be set aside due to the failure of an adopting parent, a birth parent, a birth relative, an Indian Tribe, or the child to follow the terms of this agreement or a later change to this agreement.
- A disagreement between the parties or litigation brought to enforce or modify the agreement shall not affect the validity of the adoption and shall not serve as a basis for orders affecting the custody of the child.
- A court will not act on a petition to change or enforce this agreement unless the petitioner has participated, or attempted to participate, in good faith mediation or other appropriate dispute resolution proceedings to resolve the dispute.

When a court orders that a dependent child be placed for adoption, nothing in the adoption laws of this State shall be construed to prevent the prospective adoptive parent or parents of the child from expressing a willingness to facilitate postadoptive sibling contact.

Who may be a party to a postadoption contact agreement?
Fam. Code § 8616.5; Welf. & Inst. Code § 366.29
The following persons may be parties to a postadoption contact agreement:

- The adopting parent or parents
- The birth relatives, including the birth parent or parents
- The child
- In cases governed by the Indian Child Welfare Act, the child's Indian Tribe

The child who is the subject of the adoption petition shall be considered a party to the postadoption contact agreement. A child who is age 12 or older must consent in writing to the terms and conditions of the postadoption contact agreement and any subsequent modifications unless the court finds by a preponderance of the evidence that the postadoption agreement, as written, is in the best interests of the child.

What is the role of the court in postadoption contact agreements?
Fam. Code § 8616.5; Welf. & Inst. Code § 366.29
At the time of an adoption decree, the court entering the decree may grant postadoption privileges if an agreement for those privileges has been entered into, including agreements entered into pursuant to § 8620(f) [pertaining to agreements between an Indian child and the child's Tribe].

Upon the granting of the adoption petition and the issuance of the order of adoption of a child who is a dependent of the juvenile court, juvenile court dependency jurisdiction shall be terminated. Enforcement of the postadoption contact agreement shall be under the continuing jurisdiction of the court granting the petition of adoption.

The court may not set aside an adoption decree, rescind a relinquishment, or modify an order to terminate parental rights because of the failure of any party to comply with the original terms of, or subsequent modifications to, the agreement. Exceptions are as follows:

- Prior to issuing the adoption order involving an Indian child and upon a petition of the birth or adoptive parents, birth relatives, or an Indian Tribe, the court may order the parties to engage in family mediation services to reach an agreement if the prospective adoptive parent fails to negotiate in good faith after having agreed to enter into negotiations.

- Prior to issuing the adoption order involving an Indian child, if the parties fail to negotiate in good faith to enter into an agreement during the negotiations entered into pursuant to the above paragraph, the court may modify prior orders or issue new orders as necessary to ensure the best interests of the Indian child is met. This includes, but

  is not limited to, requiring parties to engage in further family mediation services to reach an agreement, initiating guardianship proceeding in lieu of adoption, or authorizing a change of adoptive placement for the child.

Are agreements legally enforceable?
Fam. Code § 8616.5; Welf. & Inst. Code § 366.29
Enforcement of the postadoption contact agreement shall be under the continuing jurisdiction of the court granting the petition of adoption. The court may not order compliance with the agreement absent a finding that the party seeking the enforcement participated, or attempted to participate, in good faith in mediation or other appropriate dispute resolution proceedings regarding the conflict, prior to the filing of the enforcement action, and that the enforcement is in the best interests of the child.

Documentary evidence or offers of proof may serve as the basis for the court's decision regarding enforcement. No testimony or evidentiary hearing shall be required. The court shall not order further investigation or evaluation by any public or private agency or individual absent a finding by clear and convincing evidence that the best interests of the child may be protected or advanced only by that inquiry and that the inquiry will not disturb the stability of the child's home to the detriment of the child.

The court may not award monetary damages as a result of the filing of the civil action [for enforcement of the agreement].

How may an agreement be terminated or modified?
Fam. Code § 8616.5; Welf. & Inst. Code § 366.29
A postadoption contact agreement may be modified or terminated only if either of the following occurs:

- All parties, including the child if the child is age 12 or older at the time of the requested termination or modification, have signed a modified postadoption contact agreement and the agreement is filed with the court that granted the petition of adoption.

- The court finds all of the following:
  - The termination or modification is necessary to serve the best interests of the child.
  - There has been a substantial change of circumstances since the original agreement was executed and approved by the court.
  - The party seeking the termination or modification has participated, or attempted to participate, in good faith in mediation or other appropriate dispute resolution proceedings prior to seeking court approval of the proposed termination or modification.

If, following entry of an order for sibling contact, the adoptive parent(s) determine that sibling contact poses a threat to the health, safety, or well-being of the adopted child, the adoptive parent(s) may terminate the sibling contact, provided that the adoptive parent(s) must submit written notification to the court within 10 days after terminating the contact. The notification must state to the court the reasons why the health, safety, or well-being of the adopted child would be threatened by continued sibling contact.

Colorado

These issues are not addressed in the statutes reviewed.

Connecticut

What may be included in postadoption contact agreements?
Gen. Stat. § 45a-715(j), (k)
A cooperative postadoption agreement shall contain the following:

- An acknowledgment by either or both birth parents that the termination of parental rights and the adoption is irrevocable, even if the adoptive parents do not abide by the cooperative postadoption agreement
- An acknowledgment by the adoptive parents that the agreement grants either or both birth parents the right to seek enforcement of the cooperative postadoption agreement

The terms of a cooperative postadoption agreement may include the following:

- Provision for communication between the child and either or both birth parents
- Provision for future contact between either or both birth parents and the child or an adoptive parent
- Maintenance of medical history of either or both birth parents who are a party to the agreement

Who may be a party to a postadoption contact agreement?
Gen. Stat. § 45a-715(h)

Either or both birth parents and an intended adoptive parent may enter into a cooperative postadoption agreement regarding communication or contact between either or both birth parents and the adopted child. Such an agreement may be entered into if:

- The child is in the custody of the Department of Children and Families.
- An order terminating parental rights has not yet been entered.
- Either or both birth parents agree to a voluntary termination of parental rights, including an agreement in a case that began as an involuntary termination of parental rights.

The postadoption agreement shall be applicable only to a birth parent who is a party to the agreement. Such agreement shall be in addition to those under common law.

Counsel for the child and any guardian ad litem for the child may be heard on the proposed cooperative postadoption agreement. There shall be no presumption of communication or contact between the birth parents and an intended adoptive parent in the absence of a cooperative postadoption agreement.

What is the role of the court in postadoption contact agreements?
Gen. Stat. § 45a-715(i)

If the probate court determines that the child's best interests will be served by postadoption communication or contact with either or both birth parents, the court shall so order, stating the nature and frequency of the communication or contact. A court may grant postadoption communication or contact privileges if:

- Each intended adoptive parent consents to the granting of communication or contact privileges.
- The intended adoptive parent and either or both birth parents execute a cooperative agreement and file the agreement with the court.

- Consent to postadoption communication or contact is obtained from the child, if the child is at least 12 years old.
- The cooperative postadoption agreement is approved by the court.

Are agreements legally enforceable?
Gen. Stat. § 45a-715(j), (m)
A cooperative postadoption agreement shall contain the following:

- An acknowledgment by either or both birth parents that the termination of parental rights and the adoption is irrevocable, even if the adoptive parents do not abide by the cooperative postadoption agreement
- An acknowledgment by the adoptive parents that the agreement grants either or both birth parents the right to seek enforcement of the cooperative postadoption agreement

A disagreement between the parties or litigation brought to enforce or modify the agreement shall not affect the validity of the termination of parental rights or the adoption and shall not serve as a basis for orders affecting the custody of the child.

How may an agreement be terminated or modified?
Gen. Stat. § 45a-715(m), (n)
The court shall not act on a petition to change or enforce the agreement unless the petitioner had participated, or attempted to participate, in good faith in mediation or other appropriate dispute resolution proceedings to resolve the dispute.

An adoptive parent, guardian ad litem for the child, or the court on its own motion may, at any time, petition for review of communication or contact ordered by the court if the adoptive parent believes that the best interests of the child are being compromised. The court may order the communication or

Delaware

What may be included in postadoption contact agreements?
Ann. Code Tit. 13, § 929
After the placement selection process has been completed, and prior to the finalization of the adoption, identifying information may be exchanged, including, but not limited to, the exchange of names, addresses, photographs, and face-to-face meetings, provided that:

- The birth parent or parents and adoptive parent or parents request the exchange of identifying information in writing.
- The birth parent or parents and adoptive parent or parents and the Department of Services for Children, Youth and Their Families or licensed agency agree to the exchange of identifying information as specified in writing.
- The birth parent or parents and adoptive parent or parents acknowledge in writing their understanding that no legal right or assurance of continuing contact after finalization of the adoption exists.
- The birth parent or parents and adoptive parent or parents acknowledge in writing and under oath that there has been no violation of § 928 of this title.

Who may be a party to a postadoption contact agreement?
Ann. Code Tit. 13, § 929
Written consent to the exchange of identifying information must be given by the birth parent(s), adoptive parent(s), and any child age 14 or older unless the department or licensed agency deems it to be in the best interests of the child that such consent be waived.

What is the role of the court in postadoption contact agreements?
This issue is not addressed in the statutes reviewed.

Are agreements legally enforceable?
This issue is not addressed in the statutes reviewed.

How may an agreement be terminated or modified?

126 Child Welfare Information Gateway

This issue is not addressed in the statutes reviewed.

District of Columbia

What may be included in postadoption contact agreements?
Ann. Code § 4-361

A written postadoption contact agreement may allow contact after the adoption between the adopted child and a birth parent or other birth relative of the child. Written consent to the agreement must be obtained from an adopted child who is age 14 or older.

Who may be a party to a postadoption contact agreement?
Ann. Code § 4-361

The agreement is made between a prospective adoptive parent or an adoptive parent and the birth parent or other birth relative of the adopted child.

What is the role of the court in postadoption contact agreements?
Ann. Code § 4-361

The Family Court of the Superior Court of the District of Columbia must enforce an agreement if the court finds that enforcement is in the best interests of the adopted child. In enforcing an agreement, the court shall take into consideration the written consent of an adopted child who is age 14 years or older. For cases involving an adopted child who is a respondent in a child abuse or neglect case, the court finalizing the adoption shall review and approve any postadoption contact agreement based on whether it is in the best interests of the child prior to finalizing the adoption.

Are agreements legally enforceable?
Ann. Code § 4-361

Failure to comply with a condition of the postadoption agreement shall not be grounds for revoking consent to or setting aside an order for adoption.

How may an agreement be terminated or modified?
Ann. Code § 4-361

If a party to the agreement moves to modify the agreement and satisfies the court that the modification is in the best interests of the child, the court must order that the agreement be modified accordingly.

If a dispute arises between the parties to an agreement, the parties shall certify that they have participated or attempted to participate, in good faith, in mediation or other appropriate dispute resolution proceedings to resolve the dispute prior to seeking judicial resolution. The mediator shall be selected by the adoptive parent.

Florida

What may be included in postadoption contact agreements?
Ann. Stat. § 63.0427
The court may be asked to consider the appropriateness of postadoption communication or contact, including, but not limited to, visits, written correspondence, or telephone calls.

Who may be a party to a postadoption contact agreement?
Ann. Stat. § 63.0427
The child shall have the right to have contact with his or her siblings or, upon agreement of the adoptive parents, the child shall have the right to have contact with the parents who have had their parental rights terminated or other specified biological relatives.

What is the role of the court in postadoption contact agreements?
Ann. Stat. § 63.0427
The court shall consider the following in determining the appropriateness of postadoption communication:

- Any orders of the court pursuant to § 39.811(7)
- Recommendations of the Department of Children and Family Services, the foster parents if other than the adoptive parents, and the guardian ad litem
- Statements of the prospective adoptive parents
- Any other information deemed relevant and material by the court

If the court determines that the child's best interests will be served by postadoption communication or contact, the court shall so order, stating the nature and frequency of the communication or contact. This order shall be made a part of the final adoption order, but the continuing validity of the adoption may not be contingent upon such postadoption communication or contact. The ability of the adoptive parents and child to change residence within or outside the State of Florida may not be impaired by such communication or contact.

Are agreements legally enforceable?
This issue is not addressed in the statutes reviewed.

How may an agreement be terminated or modified?
Ann. Stat. § 63.0427
Notwithstanding § 63.162, the adoptive parent may, at any time, petition for review of a communication or contact order if the adoptive parent believes

128 Child Welfare Information Gateway

that the best interests of the adopted child are being compromised, and the court may order the communication or contact to be terminated or modified, as the court deems to be in the best interests of the adopted child. However, the court may not increase contact between the adopted child and siblings, birth parents, or other relatives without the consent of the adoptive parent or parents. As part of the review process, the court may order the parties to engage in mediation. The department shall not be required to be a party to such review.

Georgia

What may be included in postadoption contact agreements?
Ann. Code § 19-8-27

A postadoption contact agreement may provide for privileges regarding a child who is being adopted or who has been adopted, including, but not limited to, visitation with such child, contact with such child, sharing of information about such child, or sharing of information about birth relatives.

A postadoption contact agreement shall contain the following warnings in at least 14 point boldface type:

- After the entry of a decree for adoption, an adoption cannot be set aside due to the failure of an adopting parent, a birth parent, a birth relative, or the child to follow the terms of this agreement or a later change to this agreement.
- A disagreement between the parties or litigation brought to enforce, terminate, or modify this agreement shall not affect the validity of the adoption and shall not serve as a basis for orders affecting the custody of the child.

Who may be a party to a postadoption contact agreement?
Ann. Code § 19-8-27

An adopting parent or parents and birth relatives or an adopting parent or parents, birth relatives, and a child who is age 14 or older who is being adopted or who has been adopted may voluntarily enter into a written postadoption contact agreement to permit continuing contact between such birth relatives and such child. A child who is age 14 or older shall be considered a party to a postadoption contact agreement.

The term 'birth relative' includes:

Postadoption Contact Agreements between Birth and Adoptive ... 129

- A parent, biological father who is not the legal father, grandparent, brother, sister, half-brother, or half-sister who is related by blood or marriage to a child who is being adopted or who has been adopted
- A grandparent, brother, sister, half-brother, or half-sister who is related by adoption to a child who is being adopted or who has been adopted

What is the role of the court in postadoption contact agreements?
Ann. Code § 19-8-27

Enforcement, modification, or termination of a postadoption contact agreement shall be under the continuing jurisdiction of the court that granted the petition of adoption. However, the parties to a postadoption contact agreement may expressly waive the right to enforce, modify, or terminate such agreement.

Any party to the postadoption contact agreement may, at any time, file the original postadoption contact agreement with the court that has or had jurisdiction over the adoption if such agreement provides for the court to enforce such agreement or such agreement is silent as to the issue of enforcement.

Are agreements legally enforceable?
Ann. Code § 19-8-27

In order to be an enforceable postadoption contact agreement, the agreement shall be in writing and signed by all of the parties to such agreement acknowledging their consent to its terms and conditions.

How may an agreement be terminated or modified?
Ann. Code § 19-8-27

A postadoption contact agreement always may be modified or terminated if the parties have voluntarily signed a written modified postadoption contact agreement or termination of a postadoption contact agreement. A modified postadoption contact agreement may be filed with the court if such agreement provides for the court to enforce such agreement or such agreement is silent as to the issue of enforcement.

With respect to agreements that provide for court enforcement or termination or are silent as to such matters, any party may file a petition to enforce or terminate the agreement with the court that granted the petition of adoption, and the court shall enforce the terms of such agreement or terminate such agreement if such court finds by a preponderance of the evidence that the enforcement or termination is necessary to serve the best interests of the child.

With respect to agreements that provide for court modification or are silent as to modification, only the adopting parent or parents may file a petition seeking modification. The petition shall be filed with the court that granted the petition of adoption, and the court shall modify the agreement if the court finds by a preponderance of the evidence that the modification is necessary to serve the best interests of the child and there has been a material change of circumstances since the current postadoption contact agreement was executed.

A court may require the party seeking modification, termination, or enforcement of a postadoption contact agreement to participate in mediation or other appropriate alternative dispute resolution.

A court shall not set aside a decree of adoption, rescind a surrender, or modify an order to terminate parental rights or any other prior court order because of the failure of an adoptive parent, a birth relative, or the child to comply with any or all of the original terms of, or subsequent modifications to, a postadoption contact agreement.

Guam

These issues are not addressed in the statutes reviewed.

Hawaii

These issues are not addressed in the statutes reviewed.

Idaho

These issues are not addressed in the statutes reviewed.

Illinois

These issues are not addressed in the statutes reviewed.

Indiana

What may be included in postadoption contact agreements?
Ann. Code §§ 31-19-16-3; 31-19-16-9

A postadoption contact agreement must contain the following provisions:

- An acknowledgment by the birth parents that the adoption is irrevocable, even if the adoptive parents do not abide by the postadoption contact agreement
- An acknowledgment by the adoptive parents that the agreement grants the birth parents the right to seek enforcement of the postadoption privileges set forth in the agreement

Postadoption contact privileges are permissible without court approval in an adoption of a child who is younger than age 2 upon the agreement of the adoptive parents and a birth parent. However, postadoption contact privileges under this section may not include visitation. A postadoption contact agreement under this section is not enforceable and does not affect the finality of the adoption.

Who may be a party to a postadoption contact agreement?
Ann. Code §§ 31-19-16-1; 31-19-16.5-1

At the time an adoption decree is entered, the court entering the adoption decree may grant postadoption contact privileges to a birth parent who has consented to the adoption or voluntarily terminated the parent-child relationship.

At the time an adoption decree is entered, the court may order the adoptive parents to provide specific postadoption contact for an adopted child who is at least age 2 with a preadoptive sibling if:

- The court determines that the postadoption contact would serve the best interests of the adopted child.
- Each adoptive parent consents to the court's order for postadoption contact privileges.

What is the role of the court in postadoption contact agreements?
Ann. Code §§ 31-19-16-2; 31-19-16.5-2

A court may grant postadoption contact privileges if:

132   Child Welfare Information Gateway

- The court determines that the best interests of the child would be served.
- The child is at least age 2 and the court finds that there is a significant emotional attachment between the child and the birth parent.
- Each adoptive parent consents to the granting of postadoption contact privileges.
- The adoptive parents and the birth parents execute a postadoption contact agreement and file the agreement with the court.
- The licensed child-placing agency sponsoring the adoption and the child's court-appointed special advocate or guardian ad litem recommends to the court the postadoption contact agreement, or if there is no licensed child-placing agency sponsoring the adoption, the local office or other agency that prepared an adoption report is informed of the contents of the agreement and comments on the agreement in the agency's report to the court.
- Consent to postadoption contact is obtained from the child if the child is at least age 12.
- The postadoption contact agreement is approved by the court.

In making its determination regarding sibling postadoption contact, the court shall consider any relevant evidence, including the following:

- A recommendation made by a licensed child-placing agency sponsoring the adoption
- A recommendation made by the adopted child's court-appointed special advocate or guardian ad litem
- A recommendation made by the local office or other agency that prepared a report of its investigation and its recommendation as to the advisability of the adoption
- The wishes expressed by the adopted child or adoptive parents

Are agreements legally enforceable?
Ann. Code §§ 31-19-16-4; 31-19-16-6; 31-19-16.5-4; 31-19-16.5-5
A birth parent or an adoptive parent may file a petition with the court entering the adoption decree to compel a birth parent or an adoptive parent to comply with the postadoption contact agreement.

Before the court hears a motion to compel compliance with an agreement, the court may appoint a guardian ad litem or court- appointed special advocate to represent and protect the best interests of the child. However, the court may only appoint a guardian ad litem or court-appointed special advocate for the adopted child if the interests of an adoptive parent differ from the child's interests to the extent that the court determines that the appointment is necessary to protect the best interests of the child.

The following persons may file a petition requesting that the court vacate or modify a postadoption contact order with a preadoptive sibling or to compel an adoptive parent to comply with the postadoption contact order:

- A preadoptive sibling by a next friend, guardian ad litem, or court-appointed special advocate
- The adopted child by a next friend, guardian ad litem, or court-appointed special advocate
- An adoptive parent

How may an agreement be terminated or modified?
Ann. Code §§ 31-19-16-4; 31-19-16-6; 31-19-16.5-4; 31-19-16.5-5

A birth parent or an adoptive parent may file a petition with the court entering the adoption decree to modify the postadoption contact agreement.

The court may void or modify a postadoption contact agreement at any time before or after the adoption if the court determines after a hearing that the best interests of the child requires the voiding or modifying of the agreement.

Before the court voids or modifies an agreement, the court may appoint a guardian ad litem or court-appointed special advocate to represent and protect the best interests of the child.

The following persons may file a petition requesting that the court vacate or modify a postadoption contact order with a preadoptive sibling:

- A preadoptive sibling by a next friend, guardian ad litem, or court-appointed special advocate
- The adopted child by a next friend, guardian ad litem, or court-appointed special advocate
- An adoptive parent

The court may vacate or modify a postadoption contact order entered under this chapter at any time after the adoption if the court determines, after a hearing, that it is in the best interests of the adopted child.

Iowa

These issues are not addressed in the statutes reviewed.

Kansas

These issues are not addressed in the statutes reviewed.

Kentucky

These issues are not addressed in the statutes reviewed.

Louisiana

What may be included in postadoption contact agreements?
Children's Code Art. 1269.3

Every postadoption contact agreement shall be in writing and signed by the adopting parents and by any adult granted contact. If a sibling granted contact is a minor, his or her parent or legal custodian shall sign the agreement.

If requested by the parties, the court may refer them to mediation to assist them in drafting the agreement. If necessary to ensure that the child's best interests are taken into account, the court may also appoint independent counsel for any child involved in future continuing contact.

A continuing contact agreement may authorize the exchange of information, communication by telephone, mail, email, or other means, and direct visitation in either the adopting parents' home or elsewhere through a mutually agreed upon intermediary.

Every agreement must declare the following:

- The parties have freely and voluntarily entered into the agreement, and it reflects their intent to be bound by its terms, unless later modified by a replacement agreement or by court order.
- The sibling, grandparent, parent, or other relative by blood, adoption, or affinity has been counseled and advised by the Department of Children and Family Services, counsel, or other appropriate

professional about the meaning of the terms and the effects of a continuing contact agreement, and each has had the opportunity to have the agreement reviewed by his or her counsel.

- The sibling, grandparent, parent, or other relative has been informed and understands that upon the execution of the agreement, any dispute or litigation regarding its terms shall not affect the validity of any surrender, termination of parental rights, adoption, or custody of the adopted child.
- The adopting parents have been informed and understand that the sibling, grandparent, parent, or other relative by blood, adoption, or affinity may seek enforcement of the terms of the agreement in accordance with Article 1269.8.

Who may be a party to a postadoption contact agreement? Children's Code Art. 1264; 1269.2

In an agency adoption in which the department is the custodian of the child, the court may approve an agreement providing for continuing contact between the child to be adopted and his or his grandparent, sibling, and any parent, if both of the following conditions are met:

- The child has an established, significant relationship with that person to the extent that its loss would cause substantial harm to the child.
- The preservation of the relationship would otherwise be in the best interests of the child.

If there is no parental relationship that meets the requirements of the paragraph above, the court may approve an agreement providing for continuing contact between the child to be adopted and any other relative by blood, adoption, or affinity whose relationship with the child meets those requirements.

When adoption is approved by the court as the permanent plan for the child, the department shall inform any parent, grandparent, sibling, or any other relative or foster parent who meets the requirements above of the possibility of postadoption contact with the child upon agreement with the adoptive parents.

Notwithstanding any provision of law to the contrary, the natural parents of a deceased person whose surviving child is thereafter adopted, and the parents of a person whose parental rights have been terminated, may have limited visitation rights to the adopted minor child.

136 Child Welfare Information Gateway

What is the role of the court in postadoption contact agreements?
Children's Code Art. 1269.4; 1269.5

Within 10 days after the petition is filed, the department, attorney for the child, attorney for the parent, or attorney for the prospective adoptive parents shall file an agreement for continuing contact in the court in which the adoption is pending. The agreement may be filed later than 10 days after execution if the court agrees upon a showing of good cause.

If either the department or counsel for the child objects to the agreement, the court may conduct a hearing before approving the agreement.

The court shall review a continuing contact agreement executed in conformity with the requirements of this chapter.

If the court finds that an agreement serves the best interests of the child, the agreement shall be incorporated into a judgment of the court. An agreement reached by the parties and approved by the department and counsel representing the child is presumed to serve the best interests of the child. The judgment shall provide that failure to comply with the terms of the agreement does not constitute grounds for annulling a surrender or the final decree of adoption.

If the court rejects the agreement, it shall make specific findings of fact in support of its conclusion that the best interests of the child would not be served by approval of the agreement. The factors to be considered shall include:

- The duration of the child's relationship with the parent, grandparent, sibling, or other relative by blood, adoption, or affinity seeking continuing contact
- The strength of the psychological attachment between the child and the individual seeking continuing contact
- The resulting harm to the child if the relationship is not preserved

If the child is age 12 or older, the court shall solicit and consider the child's wishes in the matter.

Are agreements legally enforceable?
Children's Code Art. 1269.6

A continuing contact agreement shall be enforceable only if filed with the court and approved in accordance with article 1269.5.

Failure to comply with the terms of an agreement made pursuant to this chapter is not grounds for nullifying a surrender or an adoption decree or revocation by a biological parent of a surrender or consent to an adoption or for any action seeking the child's custody. Failure to include this warning in the judgment as required by article 1269.5 shall not affect the adoption.

How may an agreement be terminated or modified?
Children's Code Art. 1269.8

Unless another court has jurisdiction pursuant to the Uniform Child Custody Jurisdiction and Enforcement Act, the court shall retain jurisdiction after the decree of adoption is entered for the purpose of hearing motions brought to enforce, modify, or terminate an agreement entered into pursuant to the provisions of this chapter.

Before hearing such a motion, the court shall refer the parties to mediation. Only if the court finds that the party seeking relief has participated or attempted to participate in good faith in mediating the dispute may it proceed to a determination on the merits of the motion.

If the child is age 12 or older, the court shall solicit and consider the child's wishes in the matter.

The court shall order continuing compliance in accordance with the agreement and refuse to modify or terminate it unless it finds that there has been a change of circumstances and the agreement no longer serves the best interests of the child.

Maine

These issues are not addressed in the statutes reviewed.

Maryland

What may be included in postadoption contact agreements?
Fam. Law § 5-308

The prospective adoptive parent and the biological parent of a prospective adopted child may enter into a written agreement to allow contact after the adoption between the parent or other relative of the child and the child or adoptive parent.

An agreement made under this section applies to contact with an adopted child only while he or she is a minor.

138 Child Welfare Information Gateway

Who may be a party to a postadoption contact agreement?
Fam. Law §§ 5-308; 5-525.2
The prospective adoptive parent and birth parent may enter into a written agreement to allow contact after the adoption between:

- The parent or other relative of the adopted child
- The adopted child or adoptive parent

An adoptive parent and former parent of an adopted child may enter into a written agreement to allow contact between:

- A relative or former parent of the adopted child
- The adopted child or adoptive parent

Any siblings who are separated due to a foster care or adoptive placement may petition a court, including a juvenile court with jurisdiction over one or more of the siblings, for reasonable sibling visitation rights.

What is the role of the court in postadoption contact agreements?
Fam. Law §§ 5-308; 5-525.2
If a dispute as to an agreement arises, a court may refer the parties to mediation to try to resolve the dispute.

If a petitioner petitions a court to issue a sibling visitation decree or to amend an order, the court:

- May hold a hearing to determine whether visitation is in the best interests of the children
- Shall weigh the relative interests of each child and base its decision on the best interests of the children, thus promoting the greatest welfare and least harm to the children
- May issue an appropriate order or decree

Are agreements legally enforceable?
Fam. Law § 5-308
A juvenile court or other court of competent jurisdiction shall enforce a written agreement made in accordance with this section unless enforcement is not in the adopted child's best interests.

How may an agreement be terminated or modified?
Fam. Law § 5-308
If a party moves in juvenile court or another court of competent jurisdiction to modify a written agreement made in accordance with this

section and satisfies the court that modification is justified because an exceptional circumstance has arisen, and the court finds modification to be in an adopted child's best interests, the court may modify the agreement.

Massachusetts

What may be included in postadoption contact agreements?
Gen. Laws Ann. Ch. 210, § 6C
Prior to the entry of an adoption decree, prospective adoptive parents and a birth parent may enter into an agreement for postadoption contact or communication between or among a minor to be adopted, the prospective adoptive parents, and the birth parents.

To be approved by the court, an agreement for postadoption contact or communication must contain the following statements:

- This agreement is entered into pursuant to the provisions of Chapter 210, § 6C.
- Any breach, modification, or invalidation of the agreement or any part of it shall not affect the validity of the adoption. The adoption shall be final.
- The parties acknowledge that either the birth or adoptive parents who have entered into the agreement have the right to seek enforcement.
- The parties have not relied on any representations other than those contained in the agreement.

The agreement shall be signed by the parties and acknowledged before a notary public as the free act and deed of the parties. If the child is older than age 12, the agreement shall contain the written consent of the child. If the child is in the custody of the Department of Children and Families, the agreement shall contain the written approval of the department and the attorney for the child. If the child is in the custody of a licensed child care agency, the agreement shall contain the written approval of the agency.

Who may be a party to a postadoption contact agreement?
Gen. Laws Ann. Ch. 210, § 6C
The agreement may be between the prospective adoptive parents and the birth parents.

140 Child Welfare Information Gateway

What is the role of the court in postadoption contact agreements?

Gen. Laws Ann. Ch. 210, § 6C

The court shall approve an agreement for postadoption contact or communication if the court finds that such agreement is in the best interests of the child, contains terms that are fair and reasonable, and has been entered knowingly and voluntarily by all parties to the agreement.

The requirement that a postadoption contact agreement must be entered knowingly and voluntarily may be satisfied by an affidavit executed by all parties, either jointly or separately, that is filed with the court. The affidavit shall state that the agreement is entered into knowingly and voluntarily and is not the product of coercion or duress.

Are agreements legally enforceable?

Gen. Laws Ann. Ch. 210, §§ 6C; 6D

To be enforceable, an agreement for postadoption contact or communication shall be in writing, approved by the court prior to the date for entry of the adoption decree, incorporated but not merged into the adoption decree, and shall survive as an independent contract.

An agreement under this section need not disclose the identity of the parties to be enforceable, but if an identity is not disclosed, the unidentified person shall designate an agent for the purpose of receiving court notices.

An agreement for postadoption contact or communication shall cease to be enforceable on the date the adopted child turns age 18.

A party to a court-approved agreement for postadoption contact or communication may seek to enforce the agreement by commencing a civil action for specific performance. A court order for specific performance of the terms of a postadoption contact agreement shall be the sole remedy for breach of an agreement.

In such proceedings, parties shall not be entitled to the appointment of counsel. However, the court may appoint a guardian ad litem to represent the interests of the child.

If the court finds that an action brought under this section was wholly insubstantial, frivolous, and not advanced in good faith, the court may award attorney's fees to all prevailing parties.

Nothing in the agreement shall preclude a party seeking to enforce an agreement for postadoption contact or communication from utilizing child welfare mediation or permanency mediation before, or in addition to, the commencement of a civil action for specific enforcement.

Postadoption Contact Agreements between Birth and Adoptive ... 141

How may an agreement be terminated or modified?
Gen. Laws Ann. Ch. 210, § 6D
In an enforcement proceeding, the court may modify the terms of the agreement if the court finds that there has been a material and substantial change in circumstances and the modification is necessary in the best interests of the child. A court-imposed modification of a previously approved agreement may limit, restrict, condition, or decrease contact between the birth parents and the child, but in no event shall a court-imposed modification serve to expand, enlarge, or increase the amount of contact between the birth parents and the child or place new obligations on adoptive parents.

Michigan

These issues are not addressed in the statutes reviewed.

Minnesota

What may be included in postadoption contact agreements?
Ann. Stat. § 259.58
Adoptive parents and a birth relative or foster parents may enter an agreement regarding communication, contact, or visitation with or between a minor adopted child, adoptive parents, and a birth relative or foster parents.

Who may be a party to a postadoption contact agreement?
An agreement may be entered between:

- Adoptive parents and a birth parent
- Adoptive parents and any other birth relative or foster parent with whom the child resided before being adopted
- Adoptive parents and any other birth relative if the child is adopted by a birth relative upon the death of both birth parents

For purposes of this section, 'birth relative' means a parent, stepparent, grandparent, brother, sister, uncle, or aunt of a minor adopted child. This relationship may be by blood, adoption, or marriage. For an Indian child, birth relative includes members of the extended family as defined by the law or custom of the Indian child's Tribe or, in the absence of laws or custom, nieces,

142 Child Welfare Information Gateway

nephews, or first or second cousins, as provided in the Indian Child Welfare Act.

What is the role of the court in postadoption contact agreements?
Ann. Stat. § 259.58

An agreement regarding communication with or contact between minor adopted child, adoptive parents, and a birth relative is not legally enforceable unless the terms of the agreement are contained in a written court order entered in accordance with this section.

An order may be sought at any time before a decree of adoption is granted. The order must be issued within 30 days of being submitted to the court or by the granting of the decree of adoption, whichever is earlier.

The court shall not enter a proposed order unless the terms of the order have been approved in writing by the prospective adoptive parents, a birth relative, or foster parent who desires to be a party to the agreement and, if the child is in the custody of or under the guardianship of an agency, a representative of the agency.

A birth parent must approve in writing an agreement between adoptive parents and any other birth relative or foster parent, unless an action has been filed against the birth parent by a county under chapter 260.

An agreement under this section need not disclose the identity of the parties to be legally enforceable.

The court shall not enter a proposed order unless the court finds that the communication or contact between the minor adopted child, the adoptive parents, and a birth relative as agreed upon and contained in the proposed order would be in the minor adopted child's best interests.

Are agreements legally enforceable?
Ann. Stat. § 259.58

An agreement regarding communication with or contact between minor adopted children, adoptive parents, and a birth relative is not legally enforceable unless the terms of the agreement are contained in a written court order entered in accordance with this section.

An agreed-upon order entered under this section may be enforced by filing a petition or motion with the family court that includes a certified copy of the order granting the communication, contact, or visitation, but only if the petition or motion is accompanied by an affidavit that the parties have mediated or attempted to mediate any dispute under the agreement or that the parties agree to a proposed modification. The prevailing party may be awarded reasonable attorney's fees and costs.

Failure to comply with the terms of an agreed-upon order regarding communication or contact that has been entered by the court under this section is not grounds for:

- Setting aside an adoption decree
- Revocation of a written consent to an adoption after that consent has become irrevocable

How may an agreement be terminated or modified?
Ann. Stat. § 259.58
The court shall not modify an agreed-upon order unless it finds that the modification is necessary to serve the best interests of the minor adopted child, and:

- The modification is agreed to by the parties to the agreement.
- Exceptional circumstances have arisen since the agreement order was entered that justify modification of the order.

Mississippi

These issues are not addressed in the statutes reviewed.

Missouri

What may be included in postadoption contact agreements?
Ann. Stat. § 453.080(4)
Before the completion of an adoption, the exchange of information among the parties shall be at the discretion of the parties. Upon completion of an adoption, further contact among the parties shall be at the discretion of the adoptive parents.

Who may be a party to a postadoption contact agreement?
Ann. Stat. § 453.080(4)
The parties to the adoption may participate in the agreement.

What is the role of the court in postadoption contact agreements?
Ann. Stat. § 453.080(4)
The court shall not have jurisdiction to deny continuing contact between the adopted child and the birth parent, or an adoptive parent and a birth parent.

144   Child Welfare Information Gateway

Additionally, the court shall not have jurisdiction to deny an exchange of identifying information between an adoptive parent and a birth parent.

Are agreements legally enforceable?
This issue is not addressed in statutes reviewed.

How may an agreement be terminated or modified?
This issue is not addressed in statutes reviewed.

Montana

What may be included in postadoption contact agreements?
Ann. Code § 42-5-301
Except as otherwise provided in this title, a decree of adoption terminates any existing order or written or oral agreement for contact or communication between the adopted child and the birth parents or family.

An express written agreement entered into between the placing parent and the prospective adoptive parent after the execution of a relinquishment and consent to adoption is independent of the adoption proceedings.

Who may be a party to a postadoption contact agreement?
Ann. Code § 42-5-301
The agreement may be entered into between the placing parent and the prospective adoptive parent.

What is the role of the court in postadoption contact agreements?
Ann. Code § 42-5-301
Any express written agreement entered into between the placing parent and the prospective adoptive parent after the execution of a relinquishment and consent to adoption is independent of the adoption proceedings, and any relinquishment and consent to adopt remains valid whether or not the agreement for contact or communication is later performed. Failure to perform an agreement is not grounds for setting aside an adoption decree.

Are agreements legally enforceable?
Ann. Code § 42-5-301
The court may order that an agreement for contact or communication entered into under this section may not be enforced upon a finding that:

- Enforcement is detrimental to the child.
- Enforcement undermines the adoptive parent's parental authority.
- Due to a change in circumstances, compliance with the agreement would be unduly burdensome to one or more of the parties.

Postadoption Contact Agreements between Birth and Adoptive ... 145

How may an agreement be terminated or modified?
This issue is not addressed in the statutes reviewed.

Nebraska

What may be included in postadoption contact agreements?
Rev. Stat. §§ 43-155; 43-156; 43-157; 43-158
When planning the placement of a child for adoption, the Department of Health and Human Services may determine whether the best interests of such child might be served by placing the child in an adoption involving exchange of information.

Adoption involving exchange of information shall mean an adoption of a child in which one or both of the child's biological parents contract with the department for information about the child obtained through his or her adoptive family.

An exchange-of-information contract is a 2-year, renewable obligation, voluntarily agreed to and signed by both the adoptive and biological parent or parents as well as the department.

When the department determines that an adoption involving exchange of information would serve a child's best interests, it may enter into agreements with the child's proposed adoptive parent or parents for the exchange of information. The nature of the information promised to be provided shall be specified in an exchange-of-information contract and may include, but shall not be limited to, letters by the adoptive parent or parents at specified intervals providing information regarding the child's development or photographs of the child at specified intervals.

Any agreement shall provide that the biological parent or parents keep the department informed of any change in address or telephone number and may include provision for communication by the biological parent or parents indirectly through the department or directly to the adoptive parent or parents. Nothing in §§ 43-155 to 43-160 shall be interpreted to preclude or allow court-ordered parenting time, visitation, or other access with the biological parent or parents and the child.

Who may be a party to a postadoption contact agreement?
Rev. Stat. §§ 43-156; 43-162
An exchange-of-information contract is a 2-year, renewable obligation, voluntarily agreed to and signed by both the adoptive and biological parent or parents as well as the department.

146   Child Welfare Information Gateway

If the prospective adopted child is in the custody of the Department of Health and Human Services, the prospective adoptive parent or parents and the birth parent or parents of a prospective adopted child may enter into an agreement regarding communication or contact after the adoption between or among the prospective adopted child and his or her birth parent or parents.

What is the role of the court in postadoption contact agreements?
Rev. Stat. § 43-163

Before approving an agreement for postadoption contact, the court shall appoint a guardian ad litem to represent the best interests of the child concerning such agreement.

The court may enter an order approving the agreement upon motion of one of the child's birth parents or one of the prospective adoptive parents if the terms of the agreement are approved in writing by the prospective adoptive parents and the birth parents and if the court finds, after consideration of the recommendations of the guardian ad litem, the department, and other factors, that such communication with the birth parent or parents and the maintenance of birth family history would be in the best interests of the child.

In determining if the agreement is in the best interests of the child, the court shall consider the following factors as favoring communication with the birth parent or parents:

- Whether the child and birth parent or parents lived together for a substantial period of time
- Whether the child exhibits attachment or bonding to the birth parent or parents
- Whether the adoption is a foster parent adoption with the birth parent or parents having relinquished the prospective adopted child due to an inability to provide him or her with adequate parenting

Are agreements legally enforceable?
Rev. Stat. §§ 43-160; 43-162; 43-165

The parties to an exchange-of-information contract shall have the authority to bring suit in a court of competent jurisdiction for the enforcement of any agreement entered into pursuant to § 43-158.

Any such agreement shall not be enforceable unless approved by the court pursuant to § 43-163.

An agreement that has been approved pursuant to § 43-163 may be enforced by a civil action, and the prevailing party may be awarded reasonable attorney's fees as part of the costs of the action.

How may an agreement be terminated or modified?
Rev. Stat. §§ 43-159; 43-165
After placement of a child for adoption, the department may enter into an agreement with the biological parent or parents to alter the original contract made between the department and the biological parent or parents when it is determined by the department, in consultation with the adoptive parent or parents, that certain or all exchanges of information are no longer in the best interests of the child.

The court shall not modify an order issued under § 43-163 unless it finds that the modification is necessary to serve the best interests of the adopted child, and:

- The modification is agreed to by the adoptive parent or parents and the birth parent or parents.
- Exceptional circumstances have arisen since the order was entered that justify modification of the order.

Nevada

What may be included in postadoption contact agreements?
Rev. Stat. §§ 127.187; 127.1875
An agreement that provides for postadoptive contact is enforceable if the agreement is in writing and signed by the parties and is incorporated into an order or decree of adoption. The identity of a natural parent is not required to be included in the agreement if an agent who may receive court notices for the natural parent is provided in the agreement.

Who may be a party to a postadoption contact agreement?
Rev. Stat. § 127.187
The natural parent or parents and the prospective adoptive parent or parents of a child to be adopted may enter into an enforceable agreement that provides for postadoptive contact between:

- The child and his or her natural parent or parents
- The adoptive parent or parents and the natural parent or parents
- Any combination thereof

What is the role of the court in postadoption contact agreements?
Rev. Stat. §§ 127.187; 127.188

A court that enters an order or decree of adoption that incorporates an agreement that provides for postadoptive contact shall retain jurisdiction to enforce, modify, or terminate the agreement that provides for postadoptive contact until the child reaches 18 years of age, the child becomes emancipated, or the agreement is terminated.

The establishment of an agreement that provides for postadoptive contact does not affect the rights of an adoptive parent as the legal parent of the child.

Each prospective adoptive parent of a child to be adopted who enters into an agreement that provides for postadoptive contact shall notify the court of the existence of the agreement as soon as practicable after the agreement is established, but not later than the time at which the court enters the order or decree of adoption of the child.

Before a court may enter an order or decree of adoption of a child, the court must address in person each prospective adoptive parent, the director of the licensed child-placing agency involved in the adoption proceedings, and any attorney representing a prospective adoptive parent, the child, or the agency involved in the adoption proceedings and inquire whether the person has actual knowledge that the prospective adoptive parent or parents of the child and the natural parent of parents of the child have entered into an agreement that provides for postadoptive contact. The court may address a prospective adoptive parent by telephone.

If the court determines that the prospective adoptive parent or parents and the natural parent or parents have entered into an agreement that provides for postadoptive contact, the court shall order the prospective adoptive parent or parents to provide a copy of the agreement to the court and incorporate the agreement into the order or decree of adoption.

Are agreements legally enforceable?
Rev. Stat. §§ 127.187; 127.1885

A natural parent who has entered into an agreement that provides for postadoptive contact may, for good cause shown:

- Petition the court that entered the order or decree of adoption of the child to prove the existence of the agreement that provides for postadoptive contact and to request that the agreement be incorporated into the order or decree of adoption

- During the period set forth below, petition the court to enforce the terms of the agreement that provides for postadoptive contact if the agreement complies with the requirements of § 127.187

An adoptive parent who has entered into an agreement that provides for postadoptive contact may:

- During the period set forth below, petition the court that entered the order or decree of adoption of the child to enforce the terms of the agreement that provides for postadoptive contact if the agreement complies with the requirements of § 127.187
- Petition the court to modify or terminate the agreement that provides for postadoptive contact in the manner set forth in § 127.1895

Any action to enforce the terms of an agreement that provides for postadoptive contact must be commenced no later than 120 days after the date on which the agreement was breached.

How may an agreement be terminated or modified?
Rev. Stat. § 127.1895
An agreement that provides for postadoptive contact may only be modified or terminated by an adoptive parent petitioning the court that entered the order of decree that included the agreement. The court may grant a request to modify or terminate the agreement only if:

- The adoptive parent petitioning the court for the modification or termination establishes that:
  - A change in circumstances warrants the modification or termination.
  - The contact provided for in the agreement is no longer in the best interests of the child.
- Each party to the agreement consents to the modification or termination.

If an adoptive parent petitions the court for a modification or termination of an agreement pursuant to this section:

- There is a presumption that the modification or termination is in the best interests of the child.

150   Child Welfare Information Gateway

- The court may consider the wishes of the child involved in the agreement.

Any order issued to modify an agreement that provides postadoptive contact:

- May limit, restrict, condition, or decrease contact between the parties involved in the agreement
- May not expand or increase the contact between the parties involved in the agreement or place any new obligation on an adoptive parent

New Hampshire

What may be included in postadoption contact agreements?
Rev. Stat. § 170-B:14

Nothing in this chapter shall be construed as encouraging, discouraging, or prohibiting arrangements or understandings reached between prospective adoptive parents, birth parents, or the child-placing agency with respect to the postsurrender exchange of identifying or nonidentifying information, communication, or contact.

In adoptions involving a child who is under the legal custody of the Department of Health and Human Services, a voluntarily mediated agreement shall be enforceable as provided in this paragraph. The purpose of this paragraph is to facilitate the timely achievement of permanency for children who are in the custody of the department by providing an option for the parties to enter into a voluntarily mediated agreement for ongoing communication or contact that is in the best interests of the child, that recognizes the parties' interests and desires for ongoing communication or contact, that is appropriate given the role of the parties in the child's life, and that is legally enforceable by the courts.

An affidavit made under oath shall accompany the agreement affirmatively stating that the agreement was entered into knowingly and voluntarily and is not the product of coercion, fraud, or duress.

To be approved by the court, the agreement shall contain the following statements:

- The agreement is entered into pursuant to the provisions of § 170-B:14.
- Any breach, modification, or invalidation of the agreement, or any part of it, shall not affect the validity of the surrender of parental rights or the decree of adoption.
- The parties acknowledge that both the birth and prospective adoptive parents who have entered into the agreement have the right to seek enforcement.
- The parties have not relied on any representations other than those contained in the agreement.

The agreement shall be signed by the parties and acknowledged before a notary public as the free act and deed of the parties.

Who may be a party to a postadoption contact agreement?
Rev. Stat. § 170-B:14

Prior to the entry of any adoption decree, the department, prospective adoptive parents, and birth parents may voluntarily participate in a court-approved mediation program in order to reach a voluntarily mediated agreement.

If the department is the only party unwilling to participate in mediation, the department shall provide a written explanation of its position to the court, the birth parents, and the prospective adoptive parents.

Other people may be invited to participate in the mediation by mutual consent of the department, birth parents, and prospective adoptive parents. However, these invitees shall not be parties to any agreement reached during that mediation.

If the child who is the subject of the agreement is age 14 or older, the agreement also shall contain the written assent of the child.

What is the role of the court in postadoption contact agreements?
Rev. Stat. § 170-B:14

The court shall approve the voluntarily mediated agreement if the court determines that:

- The agreement is in the best interests of the child. In making this determination, the court may consider:
  - The length of time that the child has been under the actual care, custody, and control of any person other than a birth parent
  - The desires of the child's birth parents and the child as to the child's custody or residency

152   Child Welfare Information Gateway

- The interaction and interrelationship of the child with birth parents, siblings, and any other person who may significantly affect the child's best interests
- The adjustment to the child's home, school, and community
- The willingness and ability of the birth parents to respect and appreciate the bond between the child and the adoptive parents
- The willingness and ability of the adoptive parents to respect and appreciate the bond between the child and the birth parents
- Any evidence of abuse or neglect of the child
- The recommendations of any guardian ad litem
- An affidavit made under oath shall accompany the agreement stating that the agreement was entered into knowingly and voluntarily and is not the product of coercion, fraud, or duress.

The court issuing final approval of the agreement shall have continuing jurisdiction over enforcement of the agreement until the child reaches his or her 18th birthday.

Are agreements legally enforceable?

Rev. Stat. § 170-B:14

Except in cases involving the department, no such arrangement or understanding shall be binding or enforceable. In adoptions involving a child who is under either the legal custody or guardianship of the department, a voluntarily mediated agreement shall be enforceable as provided in this paragraph.

Any breach, modification, or invalidation of the agreement, or any part of it, shall not affect the validity of any surrender of parental rights or the interlocutory or final decree of adoption.

To be enforceable, a voluntarily mediated agreement shall be in writing, approved by the court prior to the date for entry of any adoption decree, incorporated but not merged into any adoption decree, and shall survive as an independent agreement.

A voluntarily mediated agreement need not disclose the identity of the parties to be enforceable, but if an identity is not disclosed, the unidentified person shall designate a resident agent for the purpose of service of process.

A voluntarily mediated agreement shall cease to be enforceable on the date the child turns age 18.

How may an agreement be terminated or modified?
Rev. Stat. § 170-B:14

A party to a court-approved voluntarily mediated agreement may seek to modify, enforce, or discontinue the agreement by commencing an equity action in the court that approved the agreement. However, before a court may enter an order requiring modification of, compliance with, or discontinuance of the agreement, the moving party shall certify that he or she has participated, or attempted to participate, in good faith in mediating the dispute giving rise to the action prior to filing the action. A court order for modification, enforcement, or discontinuance of the terms of the voluntarily mediated agreement shall be the sole remedies for breach of the agreement.

The court may modify the terms of the voluntarily mediated agreement if the court finds by a preponderance of the evidence that there has been a material and substantial change in the circumstances and that the modification is in the best interests of the child.

A court-imposed modification of a previously approved agreement may limit, restrict, condition, decrease, or discontinue the sharing of information and/or contact between the birth parents and the child, but in no event shall a court-imposed modification serve to expand, enlarge, or increase the amount of contact between the birth parents and the child or place new obligations on the parties to the agreement. The court also may impose appropriate sanctions consistent with its equitable powers but not inconsistent with this section, including the power to issue restraining orders.

Nothing in this section shall be construed so as to abrogate the rights of the adoptive parents to make decisions on behalf of the child, except as provided in the court-approved voluntarily mediated agreement.

New Jersey

These issues are not addressed in the statutes reviewed.

New Mexico

What may be included in postadoption contact agreements?
Ann. Stat. § 32A-5-35

An agreement for postadoption contact shall, absent a finding to the contrary, be presumed to be in the best interests of the child and shall be included in the decree of adoption.

The agreement may include contact between siblings and the adopted child on a finding that it is in the best interests of the adopted child and the adopted child's siblings and a determination that the siblings' parent, guardian, or custodian has consented.

The contact may include exchange of identifying or nonidentifying information or visitation between the parents, the parents' relatives, or the adopted child's siblings and the petitioner or visitation between the parents, the parents' relatives, or the adopted child's siblings and the adopted child. An agreement entered into pursuant to this section shall be considered an open adoption.

Every such agreement shall contain a clause that the parties agree to the continuing jurisdiction of the court and to the agreement and understand and intend that any disagreement or litigation regarding the terms of the agreement shall not affect the validity of the relinquishment of parental rights, the adoption, or the custody of the adopted child.

Who may be a party to a postadoption contact agreement?
Ann. Stat. § 32A-5-35

The parents of the adopted child and the petitioner may agree to contact between the parents and the petitioner or contact between the adopted child and one or more of the parents or contact between the adopted child and relatives of the parents.

What is the role of the court in postadoption contact agreements?
Ann. Stat. § 32A-5-35

The court may appoint a guardian ad litem for the child, particularly when visitation between the birth family and the child is included in an agreement. The court shall adopt a presumption in favor of appointing a guardian ad litem for the adopted child. However, this requirement may be waived by the court for good cause shown.

If the child is age 14 or older, the court may appoint an attorney for the child. In determining whether the agreement is in the child's best interests, the court shall consider the child's wishes, but the wishes of the child shall not control the court's findings as to the child's best interests.

Are agreements legally enforceable?
Ann. Stat. § 32A-5-35

The court shall retain jurisdiction after the decree of adoption is entered if the decree contains an agreement for contact, for the purpose of hearing motions brought to enforce or modify an agreement entered into pursuant to the provisions of this section.

How may an agreement be terminated or modified?
Ann. Stat. § 32A-5-35

The court shall not grant a request to modify the agreement unless the moving party establishes that there has been a change of circumstances and the agreement is no longer in the child's best interests.

New York

What may be included in postadoption contact agreements?
Soc. Serv. Law § 383-c(2)(b); Dom. Rel. Law § 112-b

If a child surrender instrument designates who will adopt a child, such person or persons, the child's birth parents, the authorized agency having care and custody of the child, and the child's attorney may enter into a written agreement providing for communication or contact between the child and the child's parent or parents on such terms and conditions as may be agreed to by the parties.

If the surrender instrument does not designate who will adopt the child, then the child's birth parent or parents, the authorized agency having care and custody of the child, and the child's attorney may enter into a written agreement providing for communication or contact, on such terms and conditions as may be agreed to by the parties.

Such agreement may provide terms and conditions for communication with or contact between the child and the child's biological siblings or half-siblings, if any.

Nothing in this section shall be construed to prohibit the parties to a proceeding under this chapter from entering into an agreement regarding communication with or contact between an adoptive child, adoptive parent or parents, and a birth parent or parents and/or the adoptive child's biological siblings or half-siblings.

156 Child Welfare Information Gateway

Who may be a party to a postadoption contact agreement?
Soc. Serv. Law § 383-c(2)(b); Dom. Rel. Law § 112-b

The parties to the adoption may enter into an agreement regarding communication with or contact between an adoptive child, adoptive parent or parents, and a birth parent or parents and/or the adoptive child's biological siblings or half-siblings.

If a surrender instrument designates a particular person or persons who will adopt a child, such person or persons, the child's birth parent or parents, the authorized agency having care and custody of the child, and the child's legal guardian may enter into the agreement. If a surrender instrument does not designate a particular person or persons who will adopt the child, then the child's birth parent or parents, the authorized agency having care and custody of the child, and the child's law guardian may enter into the agreement.

What is the role of the court in postadoption contact agreements?
Soc. Serv. Law § 383-c(2)(b); Dom. Rel. Law § 112-b

If the court before which the surrender instrument is presented for approval determines that the agreement concerning communication and contact is in the child's best interests, the court shall approve the agreement. If the court does not approve the agreement, the court may nonetheless approve the surrender--provided, however, that the birth parent or parents executing the surrender instrument shall be given the opportunity at that time to withdraw such instrument.

The court shall not incorporate an agreement regarding communication or contact into an order unless the terms and conditions of the agreement have been set forth in writing and consented to in writing by the parties to the agreement, including the law guardian representing the adoptive child. The court shall not enter a proposed order unless it has found that the communication with or contact between the adoptive child, the prospective adoptive parent or parents, and a birth parent or parents and/or biological siblings or half-siblings, as agreed upon and as set forth in the agreement, would be in the adoptive child's best interests.

Are agreements legally enforceable?
Soc. Serv. Law § 383-c(2)(b); Dom. Rel. Law § 112-b; Fam. Crt. Act § 1055-a

Enforcement of any agreement prior to the adoption of the child shall be in accordance with § 1055-a(b) of the family court act. Subsequent to the adoption of the child, enforcement of any agreement shall be in accordance with § 112-b of the domestic relations law.

Agreements regarding communication or contact between an adoptive child, adoptive parent or parents, and a birth parent or parents and/or biological siblings or half-siblings of an adoptive child shall not be legally enforceable unless the terms of the agreement are incorporated into a written court order. Failure to comply with the terms and conditions of an approved order regarding communication or contact that has been entered by the court pursuant to this section shall not be grounds for setting aside an adoption decree or revocation of written consent to an adoption after that consent has been approved by the court as provided in this section.

An order incorporating an agreement regarding communication or contact entered under this section may be enforced by any party to the agreement or the law guardian by filing a petition in the family court in the county where the adoption was approved.

The court shall not enforce an order under this section unless it finds that the enforcement is in the child's best interests. If an agreement for continuing contact and communication pursuant to § 383-c(2)(b) of the social services law is approved by the court, and the child who is the subject of the approved agreement has not yet been adopted, any party to the approved agreement may file a petition with the family court in the county where the agreement was approved to enforce such agreement. A copy of the approved agreement shall be annexed to such petition. The court shall enter an order enforcing communication or contact pursuant to the terms and conditions of the agreement unless the court finds that enforcement would not be in the best interests of the child.

How may an agreement be terminated or modified?
This issue is not addressed in the statutes reviewed.

North Carolina

What may be included in postadoption contact agreements?
Gen. Stat. § 48-3-610
If a person executing consent and the prospective adoptive parent or parents enter into an agreement regarding visitation, communication, support, and any other rights and duties with respect to the minor, this agreement shall not be a condition precedent to the consent itself, and failure to perform shall not invalidate a consent already given.

158   Child Welfare Information Gateway

Who may be a party to a postadoption contact agreement?
Gen. Stat. § 48-3-610
The person executing consent and the prospective adoptive parent or parents may enter into the agreement.

What is the role of the court in postadoption contact agreements?
This issue is not addressed in the statutes reviewed.

Are agreements legally enforceable?
Gen. Stat. § 48-3-610
The agreement itself shall not be enforceable.

How may an agreement be terminated or modified?
This issue is not addressed in the statutes reviewed.

North Dakota

These issues are not addressed in the statutes reviewed.

Northern Mariana Islands

These issues are not addressed in the statutes reviewed.

Ohio

What may be included in postadoption contact agreements?
Rev. Code § 3107.65
Subject to divisions (A) and (B) of this section, an open adoption may provide for the exchange of any information, including identifying information, and have any other terms. No open adoption shall do any of the following:

- Provide for the birth parent to share with the prospective adoptive parent parental control and authority over the child placed for adoption or in any manner limit the adoptive parent's full parental control and authority over the adopted child
- Deny the adoptive parent or child access to forms pertaining to the social or medical histories of the birth parent if the adoptive parent or child is entitled to them under § 3107.17

- Deny the adoptive parent or child access to a copy of the contents of the child's adoption file if the adoptive parent or child is entitled to them under § 3107.47
- Deny the adoptive parent, adopted child, birth parent, birth sibling, or other relative access to nonidentifying information that is accessible pursuant to § 3107.66, or to materials, photographs, or information that is accessible pursuant to § 3107.68
- Provide for the open adoption to be binding or enforceable

An open adoption may provide for the exchange of any information, including identifying information, and have any other terms.

Who may be a party to a postadoption contact agreement?
Rev. Code § 3107.63

A birth parent who voluntarily chooses to have the birth parent's child placed for adoption may request that the agency or attorney arranging the child's adoptive placement provide for the birth parent and prospective adoptive parent to enter into an open adoption with terms acceptable to the birth parent and prospective adoptive parent. Except as provided below, the agency or attorney shall provide for the open adoption if the birth parent and prospective adoptive parent agree to the terms of the open adoption.

An agency or attorney arranging a child's adoptive placement may refuse to provide for the birth parent and prospective adoptive parent to enter into an open adoption. If the agency or attorney refuses, the agency or attorney shall offer to refer the birth parent to another agency or attorney the agency or attorney knows will provide for open adoption.

What is the role of the court in postadoption contact agreements?
Rev. Code § 3107.65

A probate court may not refuse to approve a proposed placement pursuant to § 5103.16(D)(1) to issue a final decree of adoption or interlocutory order of adoption under § 3107.14 on the grounds that the birth parent and prospective adoptive parent have entered into an open adoption unless the court issues a finding that the terms of the open adoption violate the law or are not in the best interests of the child.

A probate court may not issue a final decree of adoption or interlocutory order of adoption that nullifies or alters the terms of an open adoption unless the court issues a finding that the terms violate the division above or are not in the best interests of the child.

Are agreements legally enforceable?
Rev. Code §§ 3107.62; 3107.65

An agency or attorney arranging a child's adoptive placement shall inform the child's birth parent and prospective adoptive parent that the birth parent and prospective adoptive parent may enter into a nonbinding open adoption in accordance with § 3107.63.

All terms of an open adoption are voluntary. Any person who has entered into an open adoption may withdraw from the open adoption at any time. An open adoption is not enforceable.

At the request of a person who has withdrawn from an open adoption, the court with jurisdiction over the adoption shall issue an order barring any other person who was a party to the open adoption from taking any action pursuant to the open adoption.

How may an agreement be terminated or modified?
Rev. Code § 3107.65

All terms of an open adoption are voluntary and any person who has entered into an open adoption may withdraw from the open adoption at any time.

Oklahoma

What may be included in postadoption contact agreements?
Ann. Stat. Tit. 10, § 7505-1.5

If a child has resided with a birth relative before being adopted, the adoptive parents and that birth relative may enter into an agreement regarding communication with, visitation of, or contact between the child, adoptive parents, and the birth relative after or during pendency of the adoption proceedings.

Who may be a party to a postadoption contact agreement?
Ann. Stat. Tit. 10, § 7505-1.5

The adoptive parents and the birth relative may enter into the agreement.

For purposes of this section, 'birth relative' means a parent, stepparent, grandparent, great-grandparent, brother, sister, uncle, or aunt of the child. This relationship may be by blood or marriage.

For an Indian child, birth relative includes members of the extended family as defined by the laws or customs of the Indian child's Tribe or, in the absence of laws or customs, shall be a person who is age 18 or older and who is the Indian child's great-grandparent, grandparent, aunt or uncle, brother or

Postadoption Contact Agreements between Birth and Adoptive ... 161

sister, brother-in-law or sister-in-law, niece, nephew, first or second cousin, or stepparent, as provided in the Indian Child Welfare Act.

What is the role of the court in postadoption contact agreements?
Ann. Stat. Tit. 10, § 7505-1.5

The court shall not enter a proposed order unless the terms of the order have been approved in writing by the prospective adoptive parents and the birth relative who desires to be a party to the agreement.

The court shall not enter a proposed order unless the court finds that the communication, visitation, or contact between the child, the adoptive parents, and the birth relative as agreed upon and contained in the proposed order would be in the child's best interests and poses no threat to the safety of the child or integrity of the adoptive placement.

Are agreements legally enforceable?
Ann. Stat. Tit. 10, § 7505-1.5

An agreement regarding communication with, visitation of, or contact between the child, adoptive parents, and a birth relative is not legally enforceable unless the terms of the agreement are contained in a written court order entered in accordance with this section.

An order must be sought and shall be filed in the adoption action.

Failure to comply with the terms of an agreed-upon order regarding communication, visitation, or contact that has been entered by the court pursuant to this section shall not be grounds for:

- Setting aside an adoption decree
- Revocation of a written consent to an adoption after that consent has become irrevocable
- An action for citation of indirect contempt of court

The prevailing party may be awarded reasonable attorney fees and costs.

How may an agreement be terminated or modified?
Ann. Stat. Tit. 10, § 7505-1.5

An agreed-upon order entered pursuant to the provisions of this section may be enforced or modified by filing a petition or motion with the court that includes a certified copy of the order granting the communication, contact, or visitation, but only if the petition or motion is accompanied by an affidavit with supporting documentation that the parties have mediated or attempted to mediate any dispute under the agreement or that the parties agree to a proposed modification.

The court shall not modify an agreed-upon order pursuant to this section unless it finds that the modification is necessary to serve the best interests of the child, and:

- The modification is agreed to by the adoptive parent and the birth relative.
- Exceptional circumstances have arisen since the agreed-upon order was entered that justify modification of the order.

Oregon

What may be included in postadoption contact agreements?
Rev. Stat. § 109.305
An adoptive parent and a birth parent may enter into a written agreement, approved by the court, to permit continuing contact between the birth relatives and the child or adoptive parents.

Who may be a party to a postadoption contact agreement?
Rev. Stat. § 109.305
An adoptive parent and a birth relative may enter into a written agreement, approved by the court, to permit continuing contact between the birth relatives and the child or adoptive parents.

As used in this subsection, the term 'birth relatives' includes birth parents, grandparents, siblings, and other members of the child's birth family. A birth relative that enters into an agreement under this subsection must have established emotional ties creating an ongoing personal relationship, as defined in § 109.119, with the child. If the child is under age 1, the ongoing personal relationship between the birth relative and the child must have continued for at least half of the child's life.

If the child is age 14 or older, an agreement made under this section may not be entered into without the consent of the child.

What is the role of the court in postadoption contact agreements?
Rev. Stat. § 109.305
The written agreement must be approved by the court.

The court may show approval of an agreement made under this section by incorporating the agreement by reference and indicating the court's approval of the agreement in the adoption judgment.

Are agreements legally enforceable?
Rev. Stat. § 109.305

An agreement made under the subsection above may be enforced by a civil action. However, before a court may enter an order requiring compliance with the agreement, the court must find that the party seeking enforcement participated, or attempted to participate, in good faith in mediating the dispute giving rise to the action prior to filing the civil action.

Failure to comply with the terms of an agreement made under this section is not grounds for setting aside an adoption judgment or revocation of a written consent to adoption.

How may an agreement be terminated or modified?
Rev. Stat. § 109.305

The court may modify an agreement if the court finds that the modification is necessary to serve the best interests of the adopted child and that:

- The party seeking modification participated, or attempted to participate, in good faith in mediation prior to seeking modification of the agreement.
- The modification is agreed to by all parties to the original agreement.
- Exceptional circumstances have arisen since the parties entered into the agreement that justify modification of the agreement.

Pennsylvania

What may be included in postadoption contact agreements?
Cons. Stat. Tit. 23, § 2731

The purpose of this subchapter is to provide an option for adoptive parents and birth relatives to enter into a voluntary agreement for ongoing communication or contact that:

- Is in the best interests of the child
- Recognizes the parties' interests and desires for ongoing communication or contact
- Is appropriate given the role of the parties in the child's life
- Is subject to approval by the courts

Who may be a party to a postadoption contact agreement?
Cons. Stat. Tit. 23, §§ 2733; 2734

A prospective adoptive parent of a child may enter into an agreement with a birth relative of the child to permit continuing contact or communication between the child and the birth relative or between the adoptive parent and the birth relative. If there are siblings who are free for adoption through the termination of parental rights following a dependency proceeding, and the prospective adoptive parent is not adopting all of the siblings, each such sibling who is younger than age 18 shall be represented by a guardian ad litem in the development of an agreement.

An agency or anyone representing the parties in an adoption shall provide notification to a prospective adoptive parent, a birth parent, and a child who can be reasonably expected to understand that a prospective adoptive parent and birth relative of a child have the option to enter into a voluntary agreement for continuing contact or communication.

If the child is age 12 years or older, an agreement may not be entered into without the child's consent.

What is the role of the court in postadoption contact agreements?
Cons. Stat. Tit. 23, § 2735

An agreement shall be filed with the court that finalizes the adoption of the child. The court shall approve the agreement if the court determines that:

- The agreement has been entered into knowingly and voluntarily by all parties. An affidavit made under oath affirmatively stating that the agreement was entered into knowingly and voluntarily and is not the product of coercion, fraud, or duress must accompany the agreement. The affidavit may be executed jointly or separately.
- The agreement is in the best interests of the child. In making that determination, the court may consider the following:
  - The circumstances of and length of time that the child has been under actual care, custody, and control of a person other than a birth parent
  - The interaction and relationships of the child with birth relatives and other persons who routinely interact with the birth relatives who may significantly affect the child's best interests
  - The adjustment to the child's home, school, and community
  - The willingness and ability of the birth relative to respect and appreciate the bond between the child and prospective adoptive parent

Postadoption Contact Agreements between Birth and Adoptive ... 165

- The willingness and ability of the prospective adoptive parent to respect and appreciate the bond between the child and the birth relative
- Any evidence of abuse or neglect of the child

Are agreements legally enforceable?
Cons. Stat. Tit. 23, §§ 2734(b); 2738; 2736
An agreement shall not be legally enforceable unless approved by the court.

Any party to an agreement, a sibling, or a child who is the subject of an agreement may seek enforcement of an agreement by filing an action in the court that finalized the adoption. That party may request only specific performance in seeking to enforce an agreement and may not request monetary damages or modification of an agreement.

For an agreement to be enforceable, it must be in writing and approved by the court on or before the date for any adoption decree. If the child is age 12 or older when the agreement is executed, the child must consent to the agreement at the time of its execution.

Before the court may enter an order enforcing an agreement, it must find all of the following:

- The party seeking enforcement of the agreement is in substantial compliance with the agreement.
- By clear and convincing evidence, enforcement serves the needs, welfare, and best interests of the child.

An agreement shall cease to be enforceable on the date the child turns age 18 unless the agreement otherwise stipulates or is modified by the court. The court issuing final approval of an agreement shall have continuing jurisdiction over enforcement of the agreement until the child turns age 18 unless the agreement otherwise stipulates or is modified by the court.

This section constitutes the exclusive remedy for enforcement of an agreement. No statutory or common law remedy is available for enforcement or damages in connection with an agreement. Failure to comply with the terms of an agreement that has been approved by the court pursuant to this subchapter shall not be grounds for setting aside an adoption decree.

How may an agreement be terminated or modified?
Cons. Stat. Tit. 23, §§ 2737; 2739

Only the adoptive parent or a child who is age 12 or older may seek to modify an agreement by filing an action in the court that finalized the adoption. Before the court may enter an order modifying the agreement, it must find by clear and convincing evidence that modification serves the needs, welfare, and best interests of the child.

A party to an agreement or a child who is at least age 12 may seek to discontinue an agreement by filing an action in the court that finalized the adoption. Before the court may enter an order discontinuing an agreement, it must find by clear and convincing evidence that discontinuance serves the needs, welfare, and best interests of the child.

Puerto Rico

These issues are not addressed in the statutes reviewed.

Rhode Island

What may be included in postadoption contact agreements?
Gen. Laws § 15-7-14.1

Postadoption privileges may include postadoption visitation, contact, and/or conveyance of information.

A postadoption privileges agreement must contain the following provisions:

- An acknowledgment by the birth parents that the adoption is irrevocable, even if the adoptive parents do not abide by the postadoption privileges agreement
- An acknowledgment by the adoptive parents that the agreement grants the birth parents the right to seek to enforce the postadoption privileges set forth in the agreement

Postadoption Contact Agreements between Birth and Adoptive ... 167

Who may be a party to a postadoption contact agreement?
Gen. Laws § 15-7-14.1

The adoptive parents and the birth parents may jointly negotiate and execute a postadoption privileges agreement that is approved and filed with the family court.

What is the role of the court in postadoption contact agreements?
Gen. Laws § 15-7-14.1

At the time an adoption decree is entered, the court entering the decree may grant postadoption visitation, contact, and/or conveyance of information privileges (hereinafter referred to as 'postadoption privileges') to a birth parent who has consented to an adoption or voluntarily terminated the parent-child relationship or has had his or her parental rights involuntarily terminated.

A court may grant postadoption privileges if:

- The court determines that the best interests of the child would be served by granting postadoption privileges.
- The court finds there is a significant emotional attachment between the child and the birth parent.
- The adoptive parents and the birth parents jointly negotiate and execute a postadoption privileges agreement that is approved and filed with the family court.
- The Department of Children, Youth, and Families and the child's court-appointed special advocate or the guardian ad litem recommend that the postadoption privileges agreement be approved by the court; or if the adoption petition is being sponsored by a licensed child-placing agency other than the department, the licensed child-placing agency sponsoring the adoption makes a recommendation that the postadoption privileges agreement be approved by the court.
- Consent to the postadoption privileges is obtained from the child if the child is at least 12 years of age.
- The postadoption privileges agreement is approved by the court.

Are agreements legally enforceable?
Gen. Laws § 15-7-14.1

A birth parent or an adoptive parent may file a petition with the court entering the adoption decree to compel a birth parent or adoptive parent to comply with the postadoption privileges agreement.

Before the court hears a motion to compel compliance with an agreement, the court shall give notice and an opportunity to be heard to the licensed, child-placing agency that sponsored the adoption and to the child's court-appointed special advocate or court- appointed guardian ad litem if one had been appointed prior to the finalization of adoption.

The court may not award monetary damages as a result of the filing of a petition under the above section.

A court may not revoke a decree of adoption because a birth parent or an adoptive parent fails to comply with a postadoption privileges agreement approved by the court.

How may an agreement be terminated or modified?
Gen. Laws § 15-7-14.1

A birth parent or an adoptive parent may file a petition with the court entering the adoption decree to modify the postadoption privileges agreement.

The court may void or modify a postadoption privileges agreement at any time before or after the adoption if the court determines after a hearing that the best interests of the child require the voiding or modification of the agreement.

Before the court voids or modifies an agreement, the court shall give notice and an opportunity to be heard to the licensed, child- placing agency that sponsored the adoption and to the child's court-appointed special advocate or court-appointed guardian ad litem if one had been appointed prior to the finalization of adoption.

South Carolina

What may be included in postadoption contact agreements?
Ann. Code § 63-9-760(D)

The validity of the final decree of adoption is not affected by an agreement entered into before the adoption between adoptive parents and biological parents concerning visitation, exchange of information, or other interaction between the child and any other person. Such an agreement does not preserve any parental rights with the biological parents and does not give to them any rights enforceable in the courts of this State.

Who may be a party to a postadoption contact agreement?
Ann. Code § 63-9-760(D)

An agreement may be made between adoptive parents and biological parents before the entry of a decree.

What is the role of the court in postadoption contact agreements?
Ann. Code § 63-9-760(D)

The validity of the final decree of adoption is not affected by an agreement entered into before the adoption between adoptive parents and biological parents concerning visitation, exchange of information, or other interaction between the child and any other person.

Are agreements legally enforceable?
Ann. Code § 63-9-760(D)

Such an agreement does not preserve any parental rights with the biological parents and does not give to them any rights enforceable in the courts of this State.

How may an agreement be terminated or modified?

This issue is not addressed in the statutes reviewed.

South Dakota

What may be included in postadoption contact agreements?
Codified Laws § 25-6-17

The natural parents of an adopted child shall retain no rights or privileges to visitation or other postadoption contact with the child, except in cases where a natural parent consents to the adoption of a child by the child's stepfather or stepmother who is the present spouse of the natural parent, or in cases of voluntary termination where there is a written preadoption agreement between the natural parent or parents and the adoptive parents.

Who may be a party to a postadoption contact agreement?
Codified Laws § 25-6-17

In cases where the natural parent consents to an adoption by the child's stepparent, or where there is a voluntary termination of the natural parent(s)' rights, the natural parents may enter into a written preadoption agreement with the adoptive parents.

What is the role of the court in postadoption contact agreements?
Codified Laws § 25-6-17

The courts do not have jurisdiction over the agreements. The South Dakota Supreme Court decision, *People in Interest of S.A.H., 537 N.W.2d 1* (S.D. 1995), is abrogated by the South Dakota Legislature insofar as the case gave circuit courts the option to order an open adoption or posttermination visitation. This section does not apply to preadoption agreements entered into before July 1, 1997.

Are agreements legally enforceable?
Codified Laws § 25-6-17

Enforcement is not specifically addressed in the statutes reviewed.

Postadoption visitation is an extraordinary remedy that may be exercised only by the adoptive parents when in the child's best interests.

How may an agreement be terminated or modified?

This issue is not addressed in the statutes reviewed.

Tennessee

What may be included in postadoption contact agreements?
Ann. Code § 36-1-121(f)

No conditions shall be placed on the adoption of the child by the adoptive parents. However, nothing under this part shall be construed to prohibit 'open adoptions' where the adoptive parents permit, in their sole discretion, the parent or guardian of the child who surrendered the child or whose rights to the child were otherwise terminated, or the siblings or other persons related to the adopted child, to visit or otherwise continue or maintain a relationship with the adopted child.

Who may be a party to a postadoption contact agreement?
Ann. Code § 36-1-121(f)

The adoptive parents have the sole discretion to permit the parent or guardian of the child, or the siblings or other persons related to the adopted child, to visit or otherwise continue or maintain a relationship with the adopted child.

What is the role of the court in postadoption contact agreements?
Ann. Code § 36-1-121(f)

The adoptive parents of a child shall not be required by any order of the adoption court to permit visitation by any other person, nor shall the order of the adoption court place any conditions on the adoption of the child by the adoptive parents. Any provision in an order of the court or in any written agreement or contract between the parent or guardian of the child and the adoptive parents requiring visitation or otherwise placing any conditions of the adoption shall be void and of no effect whatsoever; provided that nothing under this part shall be construed to prohibit 'open adoptions' where the adoptive parents permit, in their sole discretion, the parent or guardian of the child who surrendered the child or whose rights to the child were otherwise terminated, or the siblings or other persons related to the adopted child, to visit or otherwise continue or maintain a relationship with the adopted child.

Are agreements legally enforceable?
Ann. Code § 36-1-121(f)

The permission or agreement to permit visitation or contact shall not, in any manner whatsoever, establish any enforceable rights in the parent or guardian, the siblings, or other related persons.

How may an agreement be terminated or modified?

This issue is not addressed in the statutes reviewed.

Texas

What may be included in postadoption contact agreements?
Fam. Code §§ 161.2061; 161.2062

An order terminating the parent-child relationship may include terms that allow the biological parent to:

- Receive specified information regarding the child
- Provide written communications to the child
- Have limited access to the child

The order of termination may not require that a subsequent adoption order include terms regarding limited posttermination contact between the child and a biological parent.

The inclusion of a requirement for posttermination contact in a termination order does not affect the finality of a termination or subsequent adoption order or grant standing to a parent whose parental rights have been terminated to file any action under this title after the court renders a subsequent adoption order with respect to the child.

Who may be a party to a postadoption contact agreement?
Fam. Code § 161.2061

The agreement shall be between the biological parent and the Department of Protective and Regulatory Services.

What is the role of the court in postadoption contact agreements?
Fam. Code § 161.2061

If the court finds it to be in the best interests of the child, the court may provide in an order terminating the parent-child relationship that the biological parent who filed an affidavit of voluntary relinquishment of parental rights

172 Child Welfare Information Gateway

under § 161.103 shall have limited posttermination contact with the child on the agreement of the biological parent and the Department of Protective and Regulatory Services.

Are agreements legally enforceable?
Fam. Code § 161.2061

The terms of an order of termination regarding limited posttermination contact may be enforced only if the party seeking enforcement pleads and proves that, before filing the motion for enforcement, the party attempted in good faith to resolve the disputed matters through mediation.

The terms of an order of termination under this section are not enforceable by contempt.

The inclusion of a requirement for posttermination contact in a termination order does not:

- Affect the finality of a termination or subsequent adoption order
- Grant standing to a parent whose parental rights have been terminated to file any action under this title after the court renders a subsequent adoption order with respect to the child

How may an agreement be terminated or modified?
Fam. Code § 161.2061

The terms of an order of termination regarding limited posttermination contact may not be modified.

Utah

What may be included in postadoption contact agreements?
Ann. Code § 78B-6-146

A 'postadoption contact agreement' is a document, agreed upon prior to the finalization of an adoption of a child in the custody of the division, that outlines the relationship between an adoptive parent, birth parent, or other birth relative and an adopted child after the finalization of adoption.

A postadoption contact agreement shall:

- Describe:
  - Visits, if any, that shall take place between the birth parent, other birth relative, adoptive parent, and adopted child

- The degree of supervision, if any, that shall be required during a visit between a birth parent, other birth relative, and adopted child
- The information, if any, that shall be provided to a birth parent or other birth relative about the adopted child and how often that information shall be provided
- The grounds, if any, on which the adoptive parent may decline to permit visits or cease providing the information described above
- State that following the adoption, the court shall presume that the adoptive parent's judgment about the best interests of the child is correct in any action seeking to enforce, modify, or terminate the agreement

A postadoption contact agreement may not limit the adoptive parent's ability to move out of State.

Who may be a party to a postadoption contact agreement?
Ann. Code § 78B-6-146

If a child in the custody of the division is placed for adoption, the prospective adoptive parent and birth parent or other birth relative may enter into a postadoption contact agreement as provided in this section. The term 'other birth relative' means a grandparent, stepparent, sibling, stepsibling, aunt, or uncle of the prospective adoptive child.

A birth parent is not required to be a party to a postadoption contact agreement in order to permit an open adoption agreement between a prospective adoptive parent and another birth relative of the child.

What is the role of the court in postadoption contact agreements?
Ann. Code § 78B-6-146

The court that approves a postadoption contact agreement retains jurisdiction over modification, termination, and enforcement of an approved postadoption contact agreement.

Violation of an open adoption agreement is not grounds to set aside an adoption or for an award of money damages.

Nothing in this section shall be construed to mean that an open adoption agreement is required before an adoption may be finalized. Refusal or failure to agree to a postadoption contact agreement is not admissible in any adoption proceeding.

Are agreements legally enforceable?
Ann. Code § 78B-6-146

In order to be legally enforceable, a postadoption contact agreement shall be:

- Approved by the court before the finalization of the adoption, with the court making a specific finding that the agreement is in the best interest of the child
- Signed by each party claiming a right or obligation in the agreement
- Approved by the child if the adopted child is age 12 or older

In an action seeking enforcement of a postadoption contact agreement, an adoptive parent's judgment about the best interests of the child is entitled to a presumption of correctness. If the party seeking to enforce the postadoption contact agreement successfully rebuts that presumption, the court shall consider whether:

- The parties performed the duties outlined in the open adoption agreement in good faith.
- There is a reasonable alternative that fulfills the spirit of the open adoption agreement without ordering mandatory compliance with the open adoption agreement.
- Enforcement of the open adoption agreement is in the best interests of the adopted child.

The court shall order the parties to attend mediation if the presumption of the correctness of the adoptive parent's judgment is successfully rebutted, and mediation is in the child's best interests.

An open adoption agreement that has been found not to be in the best interests of the adopted child shall not be enforced.

How may an agreement be terminated or modified?
Ann. Code § 78B-6-146

A postadoption contact agreement may be modified only with the consent of the adoptive parent.

Vermont

What may be included in postadoption contact agreements?
Ann. Stat. Tit. 15A, § 4-112
[This section applies to stepparent adoptions only.]

Upon the request of the petitioner, the petitioner's spouse, the child's other parent, or a relative of the child, the court shall review a written agreement that permits another person to visit or communicate with the minor after the decree of adoption becomes final.

Who may be a party to a postadoption contact agreement?
Ann. Stat. Tit. 15A, § 4-112
[This section applies to stepparent adoptions only.]

The agreement shall be signed by the person, the petitioner, the petitioner's spouse, the minor if age 14 or older, and, if an agency placed the minor for adoption, an authorized employee of the agency.

What is the role of the court in postadoption contact agreements?
Ann. Stat. Tit. 15A, § 4-112
[This section applies to stepparent adoptions only.]

The court may enter an order approving an agreement only upon determining that the agreement is in the best interests of the child. In making this determination, the court shall consider:

- The preference of the child, if the child is mature enough to express a preference
- Any special needs of the child and how they would be affected by performance of the agreement
- The length and quality of any existing relationship between the child and the person who would be entitled to visit or communicate and the likely effect on the child of allowing this relationship to continue
- The specific terms of the agreement and the likelihood that the parties to the agreement will cooperate in performing its terms
- The recommendation of the child's guardian ad litem, attorney, social worker, or other counselor
- Any other factor relevant to the best interests of the child

176 Child Welfare Information Gateway

In addition to any agreement approved pursuant to this section, the court may approve the continuation of an existing order or issue a new order permitting the child's former parent, grandparent, or sibling to visit or communicate with the minor if:

- The grandparent is the parent of a deceased parent of the child or the parent of the child's parent whose parental relationship to the child is terminated by the decree of adoption.
- The former parent, grandparent, or sibling requests that an existing order be permitted to survive the decree of adoption or that a new order be issued.
- The court determines that the requested visitation or communication is in the best interests of the child.

In making its determination, the court shall consider the factors listed above and any objections to the requested order by the adoptive stepparent and the stepparent's spouse.

Are agreements legally enforceable?

Ann. Stat. Tit. 15A, §§ 1-109; 4-112

When a decree of adoption becomes final, except as provided in article 4 of this title, any order or agreement for visitation or communication with the minor shall be unenforceable.

In the case of a stepparent adoption, an order issued [for visitation] may be enforced in a civil action only if the court finds that enforcement is in the best interests of a child.

Failure to comply with the terms of an order in a stepparent adoption or with any other agreement for visitation or communication is not a ground for revoking, setting aside, or otherwise challenging the validity of a consent, relinquishment, or adoption pertaining to a minor stepchild, and the validity of the consent, relinquishment, and adoption is not affected by any later action to enforce, modify, or set aside the order or agreement.

How may an agreement be terminated or modified?

Ann. Stat. Tit. 15A, § 4-112

[This section applies to stepparent adoptions only.]

An order issued under this section may not be modified unless the court finds that modification is in the best interests of a child, and:

Postadoption Contact Agreements between Birth and Adoptive ... 177

- The persons subject to the order request the modification.
- Exceptional circumstances arising since the order was issued justify the modification.

Virgin Islands

These issues are not addressed in the statutes reviewed.

Virginia

What may be included in postadoption contact agreements?
Ann. Code § 63.2-1220.2

A postadoption contact and communication agreement may include, but is not limited to, provisions related to contact and communication between the child, the birth parents, and the adoptive parents and provisions for the sharing of information about the child, including sharing of photographs of the child and information about the child's education, health, and welfare.

Any postadoption contact and communication agreement shall include acknowledgment by the birth parents that the adoption of the child is irrevocable, even if the adoptive parents do not abide by the postadoption contact and communication agreement, and acknowledgment by the adoptive parents that the agreement grants the birth parents the right to seek to enforce the provisions set forth in the agreement. The petitioner for adoption shall file the agreement with other documents filed in the circuit court having jurisdiction over the child's adoption.

Who may be a party to a postadoption contact agreement?
Ann. Code §§ 16.1-283.1; 63.2-1220.2

In any case in which a child has been placed in foster care as a result of court commitment, an entrustment agreement entered into by the parent(s), or other voluntary relinquishment by the parent(s), the child's birth parent(s) may enter into a written postadoption contact and communication agreement with the preadoptive parent(s).

In any proceeding for adoption pursuant to Chapter 12, the birth parent(s) and the adoptive parent(s) of a child may enter into a written postadoption contact and communication agreement.

What is the role of the court in postadoption contact agreements?
Ann. Code §§ 16.1-283.1; 63.2-1220.3; 63.2-1220.4

The court may consider the appropriateness of a written postadoption contact and communication agreement at the permanency planning hearing and, if the court finds that all of the requirements of § 16.1-283.1(A) and § 63.2-1220.2, et seq., have been met, shall incorporate the written postadoption contact and communication agreement into an order entered at the conclusion of the hearing.

The circuit court may approve a postadoption contact and communication agreement authorized pursuant to § 16.1-283.1 and filed with the court for a petition for adoption if:

- The court determines that the child's best interests would be served by approving the postadoption contact and communication agreement.
- The adoptive parent or parents and birth parent or parents have consented to a postadoption contact and communication agreement filed with the court.
- The agency authorized to consent to the child's adoption and the child's guardian ad litem have recommended that the postadoption contact and communication agreement be approved as being in the best interests of the child, or, if there is no agency sponsoring the adoption, the agency that prepared the adoption report has been informed of the postadoption contact and communication agreement and has recommended in the agency's report to the circuit court that the postadoption contact and communication agreement be approved.
- The adoptive child who is age 14 or older consents to the postadoption contact and communication agreement.

The circuit court shall not require execution of a postadoption contact and communication agreement as a condition for approving any adoption.

Unless otherwise stated in the final order of adoption, the circuit court of the jurisdiction in which the final order of adoption was entered shall retain jurisdiction to modify or enforce the terms of a postadoption contact and communication agreement.

Are agreements legally enforceable?
Ann. Code §§ 63.2-1220.3; 63.2-1220.4

To be enforceable, any agreement under this section shall be approved by the circuit court and incorporated into the final order of adoption.

A birth parent or adoptive parent who has executed a postadoption contact and communication agreement may file a petition with the circuit court of the jurisdiction in which the final order of adoption was entered to compel a birth or adoptive parent to comply with the postadoption contact and communication agreement. The court may not award monetary damages as a result of the filing of a petition for compliance with the agreement.

Before the court hears a motion to compel compliance, the court may appoint a guardian ad litem to represent the child's best interests.

The court may not award monetary damages as a result of the filing of a petition for modification of or compliance with the agreement.

How may an agreement be terminated or modified?
Ann. Code § 63.2-1220.4

Unless otherwise stated in the final order of adoption, the circuit court of the jurisdiction in which the final order of adoption was entered shall retain jurisdiction to modify or enforce the terms of a postadoption contact and communication agreement.

A birth parent or parents or adoptive parent or parents who have executed a postadoption contact and communication agreement may file a petition with the court to modify the postadoption contact and communication agreement or compel a birth or adoptive parent to comply with the postadoption contact and communication agreement.

The court may not award monetary damages as a result of the filing of a petition for modification of the agreement. The court may modify the agreement at any time before or after the adoption if the court, after notice and opportunity to be heard by the birth parent or parents and the adoptive parent or parents, determines that the child's best interests require the modification of the agreement. Before the court modifies an agreement or hears a motion to compel compliance, the court may appoint a guardian ad litem to represent the child's best interests.

The court shall not grant a request to modify the terms of a postadoption contact and communication agreement unless the moving party establishes that there has been a change of circumstances and the agreement is no longer in the child's best interests. No modification shall affect the irrevocability of the adoption.

Washington

What may be included in postadoption contact agreements?
Rev. Code §§ 26.33.295; 26.33.420; 26.33.430

Nothing in this chapter shall be construed to prohibit the parties to a proceeding under this chapter from entering into agreements regarding communication with or contact between adopted children, adoptive parents, siblings of adopted children, and a birth parent or parents.

An agreement under this section need not disclose the identity of the parties to be legally enforceable.

The legislature intends to promote a greater focus, in permanency planning and adoption proceedings, on the interests of siblings separated by adoptive placements and to encourage the inclusion in adoption agreements of provisions to support ongoing postadoption contact between siblings.

To the extent feasible, and when in the best interests of the adopted child and siblings of the adopted child, contact between the siblings should be frequent and of a similar nature as that which existed prior to the adoption.

Who may be a party to a postadoption contact agreement?
Rev. Code §§ 26.33.295; 26.33.430

An agreement may entered into between the adoptive parents and the birth parents.

The court, in reviewing and approving an agreement under § 26.33.295 for the adoption of a child from foster care, shall encourage the adoptive parents, birth parents, foster parents, kinship caregivers, and the Department of Social and Health Services or other supervising agency to seriously consider the long-term benefits to the adopted child and siblings of the adopted child of providing for and facilitating continuing postadoption contact between siblings.

What is the role of the court in postadoption contact agreements?
Rev. Code §§ 26.33.295; 26.33.430

The court shall not enter a proposed order unless the terms of such order have been approved in writing by the prospective adoptive parents, any birth parent whose parental rights have not previously been terminated, and, if the child is in the custody of the department or a licensed child-placing agency, a representative of the department or child-placing agency. If the child is represented by an attorney or guardian ad litem in a proceeding under this chapter or in any other child-custody proceeding, the terms of the proposed order also must be approved in writing by the child's representative. An agreement under this section need not disclose the identity of the parties to be legally enforceable.

The court shall not enter a proposed order unless the court finds that the communication or contact between the adopted child, the adoptive parents, and a birth parent or parents as agreed upon and as set forth in the proposed order would be in the adopted child's best interests.

If the adopted child or known siblings of the adopted child are represented by an attorney or guardian ad litem in a proceeding under this chapter or in any other child custody proceeding, the court shall inquire of each attorney and guardian ad litem regarding the potential benefits of continuing contact between the siblings and the potential detriments of severing contact.

Are agreements legally enforceable?

Rev. Code § 26.33.295

Agreements regarding communication with or contact between adopted children, adoptive parents, and a birth parent or parents shall not be legally enforceable unless the terms of the agreement are set forth in a written court order entered in accordance with the provisions of this section.

An agreement may be enforced by a civil action, and the prevailing party in that action may be awarded, as part of the costs of the action, a reasonable amount to be fixed by the court as attorney fees.

An agreement under this section need not disclose the identity of the parties to be legally enforceable.

Failure to comply with the terms of an agreed-upon order regarding communication or contact that has been entered by the court pursuant to this section shall not be grounds for setting aside an adoption decree or revocation of a written consent to an adoption after that consent has been approved by the court as provided in this chapter.

How may an agreement be terminated or modified?

Rev. Code § 26.33.295

The court shall not modify an agreed-upon order under this section unless it finds that the modification is necessary to serve the best interests of the adopted child, and that:

- The modification is agreed to by the adoptive parent and the birth parent or parents.
- Exceptional circumstances have arisen since the agreed-upon order was entered that justify modification of the order.

West Virginia

What may be included in postadoption contact agreements?
This issue is not addressed in the statutes reviewed.
Who may be a party to a postadoption contact agreement?
This issue is not addressed in the statutes reviewed.
What is the role of the court in postadoption contact agreements?
Ann. Code § 48-22-704
A decree or order entered under this article may not be vacated or set aside upon application of a person alleging that there is a failure to comply with an agreement for visitation or communication with the adopted child.
Are agreements legally enforceable?
Ann. Code § 48-22-704
The court may hear a petition to enforce the agreement, in which case the court shall determine whether enforcement of the agreement would serve the best interests of the child. The court may, in its sole discretion, consider the position of a child of the age and maturity to express such position to the court.
How may an agreement be terminated or modified?
This issue is not addressed in the statutes reviewed.

Wisconsin

What may be included in postadoption contact agreements?
This issue is not addressed in the statutes reviewed.
Who may be a party to a postadoption contact agreement?
Ann. Stat. § 48.925(1)
[This section applies to stepparent and relative adoptions only.]
Upon petition by a relative who has maintained a relationship similar to a parent-child relationship with a child who has been adopted by a stepparent or relative, the court may grant reasonable visitation rights to that person if the petitioner has maintained such a relationship within 2 years prior to the filing of the petition.
What is the role of the court in postadoption contact agreements?
Ann. Stat. § 48.925(1)-(3)
The adoptive parent or parents, or, if a birth parent is the spouse of an adoptive parent, the adoptive parent and birth parent, shall have notice of the hearing. The court will determine all of the following:

Postadoption Contact Agreements between Birth and Adoptive ... 183

- That visitation is in the best interests of the child
- That the petitioner will not undermine the adoptive parent(s) relationship with the child
- That the petitioner will not act in a manner contrary to parenting decisions related to the child's physical, emotional, educational, or spiritual welfare made by the adoptive parent(s)

The court may not grant visitation rights to a relative if the relative has been convicted of the intentional homicide of a parent of the child, and the conviction has not been reversed, set aside, or vacated. If a relative who is granted visitation rights with a child is convicted of the intentional homicide of a parent of the child, and the conviction has not been reversed, set aside, or vacated, the court shall issue an order prohibiting the relative from having visitation with the child on petition of the child or the parent, guardian, or legal custodian of the child, or on the court's own motion, and on notice to the relative. These provisions do not apply if the court determines by clear and convincing evidence that the visitation would be in the best interests of the child. The court shall consider the wishes of the child in making that determination.

Whenever possible, in making a determination of visitation with a relative, the court shall consider the wishes of the adopted child. This section applies to every child in this State who has been adopted by a stepparent or relative, regardless of the date of the adoption.

Are agreements legally enforceable?

Ann. Stat. § 48.925(4)

Any person who interferes with visitation rights granted under this section may be proceeded against for contempt of court, except that a court may impose only the remedial sanctions against that person.

How may an agreement be terminated or modified?

This issue is not addressed in the statutes reviewed.

Wyoming

These issues are not addressed in the statutes reviewed.

184   Child Welfare Information Gateway

End Notes

[1] For more information on the issue of postadoption contact, see the Information Gateway publication Openness in Adoption: Building Relationships Between Adoptive and Birth Families at https://www. childwelfare.gov/pubs/f_openadopt.cfm.

[2] The word "approximately" is used to stress the fact that States frequently amend their laws; this information is current through June 2014. States that permit enforceable contracts include Alaska, Arizona, California, Connecticut, Florida, Georgia, Indiana (for children over age 2), Louisiana, Maryland, Massachusetts, Minnesota, Montana, Nebraska, Nevada, New Hampshire (enforceable agreements only in relation to children in the custody of the Department of Health and Human Services), New Mexico, New York, Oklahoma, Oregon, Pennsylvania, Rhode Island, Texas, Utah, Vermont (stepparent adoptions only), Virginia, Washington, West Virginia, and Wisconsin (stepparent and relative adoptions only).

[3] The phrase "parties to an adoption" generally refers to the birth parents (or other person placing the child for adoption) and the adoptive parents; it may include the adoptive child under the laws of some States.

[4] Contact agreements may include visits between siblings in California, Georgia, Louisiana, Minnesota, New Mexico, New York, Oklahoma, Oregon, Pennsylvania, Tennessee, Utah, and Washington. Courts also may order visitation for siblings outside of contact agreements between the birth and adoptive parents.

[5] California, Connecticut, Indiana, Massachusetts, Pennsylvania, Rhode Island, and Utah.

[6] Delaware, Georgia, New Hampshire, Oregon, Vermont (which requires the child to sign the agreement if he or she is older than age 14), and Virginia.

[7] Arizona, California, Connecticut, Louisiana, Minnesota, New Hampshire, Oklahoma, Oregon, and Texas.

INDEX

A

abuse, 41, 47, 48, 97, 152, 164

adopted persons, vii, 3, 5, 24, 27, 30, 39, 41, 55, 61, 75, 85, 87, 89, 95, 109

adoption records, vii, 1, 2, 3, 4, 5, 14, 15, 16, 26, 37, 39, 46, 52, 53, 74, 92, 108

adoptive parents, vii, 3, 4, 5, 6, 9, 10, 11, 18, 20, 21, 22, 23, 24, 26, 29, 30, 36, 37, 38, 39, 40, 41, 43, 45, 46, 47, 50, 54, 58, 60, 62, 66, 69, 70, 71, 72, 79, 86, 87, 90, 92, 94, 99, 100, 103, 112, 115, 117, 118, 120, 122, 123, 124, 127, 131, 132, 136, 139, 140, 141, 142, 143, 146, 150, 151, 152, 153, 160, 161, 162, 163, 166, 167, 168, 169, 170, 176, 177, 179, 180, 183

agencies, 25, 80, 99

Alaska, 8, 9, 109, 116, 183

American Samoa, 2, 5, 9, 10, 108, 117

B

background information, 37, 66

C

certificate, 1, 5, 7, 9, 11, 12, 13, 14, 16, 17, 19, 21, 23, 25, 27, 28, 30, 31, 33, 35, 36, 37, 38, 40, 41, 42, 44, 49, 53, 54, 55, 56, 57, 59, 60, 61, 63, 64, 65, 67, 69, 70, 71, 73, 78, 80, 81, 84, 85, 86, 88, 89, 92, 94, 95, 96, 98, 100, 102, 104, 107, 108

child abuse, 126

child-placing agency, 3, 7, 9, 15, 17, 19, 22, 23, 24, 28, 32, 41, 44, 48, 51, 55, 58, 59, 60, 62, 69, 70, 72, 92, 93, 132, 148, 150, 167, 180

children, 2, 8, 10, 11, 18, 27, 29, 30, 31, 72, 86, 89, 111, 113, 138, 142, 150, 179, 180, 183

civil action, 121, 140, 141, 147, 162, 176, 180

communication, 78, 111, 112, 113, 117, 123, 124, 125, 127, 128, 134, 139, 140, 142, 143, 144, 145, 146, 150, 155, 156, 157, 160, 161, 163, 175, 176, 177, 178, 179, 180, 181

compliance, 88, 114, 121, 133, 137, 145, 153, 162, 165, 167, 174, 178, 179

confidentiality, 3, 26, 39, 42, 49, 50, 82, 83, 97

consent, 1, 3, 4, 5, 7, 10, 12, 13, 14, 15, 16, 17, 20, 22, 23, 24, 26, 27, 28, 32, 33, 34, 35, 37, 48, 49, 50, 51, 55, 57, 58, 59, 61, 66, 68, 70, 73, 78, 84, 89, 91, 92, 93, 96, 97, 100, 101, 102, 103, 104, 108, 109, 114, 117, 118, 120, 125, 126, 128, 129, 137, 139, 143, 144, 151, 156, 157, 161, 162, 164, 165, 174, 176, 177, 181

cooperative adoption, vii, 111

counsel, 134, 135, 136, 140
counseling, 3, 12, 41, 50, 53, 88, 93, 104
court approval, 26, 122, 131

D

damages, 121, 165, 167, 173, 178, 179
denial, 75, 76, 95
Department of Health and Human Services, 1, 58, 60, 71, 111, 145, 146, 150, 183
disability, 80, 104
disclosure, 3, 7, 8, 10, 11, 13, 24, 30, 34, 35, 39, 44, 46, 49, 50, 51, 56, 57, 62, 72, 73, 84, 88, 90, 93, 97, 98, 99, 100, 101, 104, 107
diseases, 26, 52, 63, 107
District of Columbia, 5, 21, 108, 112, 114, 126

E

education, 29, 72, 176
emotional health, 3, 19, 24
enforcement, 114, 116, 121, 123, 124, 126, 129, 130, 131, 135, 138, 139, 141, 146, 151, 152, 153, 156, 157, 162, 165, 171, 173, 176, 181
enrollment, 51, 66, 73
ethnic background, 8, 26, 29, 67, 70, 75, 89, 90, 91
evidence, 3, 7, 50, 95, 104, 116, 120, 121, 130, 132, 152, 153, 164, 165, 166, 182
execution, 135, 136, 144, 165, 178

F

families, vii, 10, 30, 66, 70, 111
family history, 64, 146
family members, 4, 64, 74, 101, 109, 112
foster parent, vii, 48, 97, 111, 113, 127, 135, 141, 142, 146, 179

G

genetic information, 27, 39, 40, 41, 52, 105
Georgia, 3, 23, 25, 109, 114, 128, 183
grants, 123, 124, 131, 166, 177
Guam, 2, 5, 25, 108, 130
guardian, 2, 10, 11, 14, 18, 23, 26, 28, 29, 30, 40, 41, 52, 53, 65, 70, 73, 77, 79, 80, 81, 83, 84, 90, 92, 94, 96, 98, 103, 105, 106, 123, 125, 127, 132, 133, 140, 146, 152, 154, 156, 157, 163, 167, 168, 170, 175, 177, 178, 179, 180, 182

H

Hawaii, 25, 109, 130
health, 2, 3, 6, 10, 11, 19, 20, 23, 24, 36, 37, 41, 43, 47, 50, 62, 63, 64, 66, 67, 69, 70, 72, 79, 85, 86, 87, 89, 90, 91, 94, 97, 103, 107, 122, 176
Health and Human Services, 56, 57
health information, 3, 20, 50, 70, 90, 91
history, 2, 7, 10, 11, 13, 15, 16, 18, 19, 22, 23, 24, 34, 37, 41, 42, 43, 47, 49, 52, 58, 59, 60, 62, 64, 67, 70, 72, 74, 77, 79, 82, 83, 84, 85, 86, 89, 92, 93, 94, 97, 101, 103, 106, 107

I

identification, 3, 15, 30, 32, 42, 60, 63, 89, 95, 100
identifying information, vii, 1, 3, 4, 5, 6, 7, 10, 11, 16, 19, 20, 21, 22, 24, 27, 30, 31, 32, 33, 34, 37, 43, 44, 48, 49, 50, 51, 53, 55, 56, 57, 58, 59, 62, 63, 65, 66, 68, 69, 70, 72, 73, 74, 75, 77, 78, 79, 80, 82, 83, 84, 86, 89, 95, 96, 97, 98, 99, 100, 101, 102, 104, 106, 108, 109, 125, 144, 158, 159
identity, 3, 6, 9, 13, 19, 24, 32, 34, 35, 37, 40, 41, 45, 46, 53, 56, 66, 71, 73, 78, 84, 87, 91, 93, 101, 104, 105, 106, 118, 140, 142, 147, 152, 179, 180

Index

187

informal practices, 6, 115
intermediaries, 16, 107, 109
Iowa, 34, 35, 109, 134

J

jurisdiction, 47, 51, 65, 88, 105, 113, 117, 118, 120, 121, 129, 137, 138, 139, 144, 146, 148, 152, 154, 160, 165, 169, 173, 177, 178

L

laws, 1, 5, 108, 112, 119, 142, 160, 183
lineal descendants, 54, 55, 90
litigation, 119, 124, 128, 135, 154
Louisiana, 38, 40, 108, 109, 114, 134, 183

M

majority, 22, 98, 107
marriage, 13, 129, 141, 160
Maryland, 3, 43, 45, 108, 109, 114, 137, 183
mediation, 112, 114, 119, 120, 121, 122, 124, 127, 128, 130, 134, 137, 138, 141, 151, 163, 171, 174
medical, 2, 3, 6, 7, 8, 13, 14, 16, 17, 19, 20, 22, 23, 24, 25, 26, 27, 29, 30, 32, 34, 36, 39, 41, 42, 43, 46, 47, 48, 49, 50, 52, 54, 58, 59, 60, 62, 63, 64, 66, 69, 74, 75, 76, 77, 78, 81, 83, 84, 86, 87, 96, 102, 104, 105, 107, 108, 109, 112, 123, 158
medical history, 2, 6, 7, 8, 13, 16, 17, 22, 34, 42, 50, 54, 58, 59, 63, 64, 75, 76, 81, 86, 87, 96, 107, 123
medical information, 3, 20, 23, 24, 26, 30, 39, 43, 62, 69, 78, 107, 109
medication, 41, 107
membership, 8, 51, 80
mental health, 29, 43, 50, 90, 91, 93
Mexico, 65, 67, 108, 109, 114, 153, 183
Missouri, 54, 55, 109, 115, 143
modifications, 120, 130

Montana, 56, 57, 108, 109, 144, 183

N

nationality, 18, 54, 67, 70, 89
neglect, 14, 47, 48, 126, 152, 164
nonidentifying information, 1, 2, 6, 8, 9, 15, 16, 19, 20, 22, 23, 24, 29, 30, 46, 52, 56, 63, 65, 67, 68, 70, 74, 77, 82, 83, 87, 91, 97, 101, 103, 108, 150, 154, 158

O

Oklahoma, 2, 77, 79, 108, 109, 113, 160, 183
open adoption, vii, 111, 154, 158, 159, 160, 169, 170, 173, 174

P

parental authority, 144
parental control, 158
parent-child relationship, 131, 166, 171, 182
parenting, 145, 146, 182
personal communication, 108
personal relationship, 162
personality, 63, 90
photographs, 20, 125, 145, 158, 176
postadoption contact agreements, vii, 114, 115, 116, 117, 119, 120, 122, 124, 125, 126, 127, 128, 129, 131, 132, 134, 136, 137, 138, 139, 140, 141, 142, 143, 144, 145, 146, 147, 148, 150, 151, 153, 154, 155, 156, 157, 158, 159, 160, 162, 163, 164, 166, 168, 169, 170, 171, 172, 173, 174, 176, 177, 179, 180, 181, 182
pregnancy, 41, 47, 63, 107
Puerto Rico, 5, 84, 108, 166

R

race, 29, 67, 70, 89, 90, 91
recommendations, 146, 152

Registry(ies), 1, 4, 11, 12, 23, 25, 27, 28, 29, 30, 31, 33, 35, 40, 42, 44, 45, 55, 61, 65, 69, 79, 81, 84, 85, 86, 88, 89, 92, 94, 98, 105
regulations, 6, 73, 115
relatives, 2, 3, 5, 8, 12, 16, 18, 24, 29, 30, 37, 59, 62, 72, 85, 89, 90, 91, 102, 111, 112, 113, 115, 116, 119, 120, 127, 128, 129, 154, 162, 163, 164
religion, 2, 8, 29, 67, 72, 75, 89
requirement, 140, 154, 171
requirements, 42, 44, 135, 136, 149, 177
resolution, 119, 121, 122, 124, 127, 130
rights, 7, 18, 39, 48, 55, 66, 82, 84, 89, 93, 111, 113, 114, 115, 116, 117, 118, 120, 122, 123, 124, 127, 130, 135, 136, 138, 148, 151, 152, 153, 154, 157, 163, 166, 168, 169, 170, 171, 172, 180, 182, 183

47, 48, 52, 55, 65, 67, 68, 69, 70, 72, 73, 74, 75, 77, 78, 79, 80, 81, 82, 85, 86, 90, 92, 93, 94, 95, 96, 98, 99, 102, 103, 107, 120, 122, 131, 132, 133, 134, 135, 136, 138, 155, 156, 158, 162, 163, 165, 173, 175, 179, 180, 183
South Dakota, 88, 89, 109, 115, 169
special education, 47, 97
stability, 121
state, vii, 1, 33, 42, 86, 112, 114, 115, 117, 122, 140
statutes, 2, 3, 21, 33, 73, 84, 98, 112, 113, 114, 115, 117, 118, 122, 126, 128, 130, 131, 134, 137, 141, 143, 144, 145, 153, 157, 158, 166, 168, 169, 170, 176, 181, 183
Supreme Court, 11, 169

S

safety, 63, 113, 122, 161
sanctions, 153, 183
school, 8, 48, 89, 97, 101, 152, 164
services, 23, 28, 50, 60, 70, 77, 88, 99, 105, 121
showing, 23, 40, 100, 116, 136
sibling(s), 2, 3, 14, 15, 18, 21, 22, 23, 24, 27, 28, 29, 34, 35, 37, 38, 39, 40, 41, 43,

W

waiver, 4, 14, 93, 97
Washington, 100, 102, 108, 109, 179, 183
welfare, 11, 21, 25, 60, 138, 141, 165, 166, 176, 182
well-being, 75, 122
Wisconsin, 105, 107, 109, 113, 181, 183